# SCHOLASTIC
# LITERACY
# PLACE

## IT WORKS...AND KIDS LIKE IT!

**SCHOLASTIC**

# SCHOLASTIC
# LITERACY PLACE

## IT WORKS...AND KIDS LIKE IT!

### Manageable Instructional Plans

Literacy Place follows a clear, consistent pattern of

instruction and provides support for all learners. The

Teacher's Edition includes explicit skills instruction and

integrates the language arts.

### The Strongest System for Beginning Readers

Literacy Place provides direct instruction in phonics and

phonological awareness and fully reflects current and

confirmed research.

## Assessment Tools to Monitor and Modify Instruction

Literacy Place features focused assessment that informs

instruction and measures progress. The program offers

strategies targeting students who need skills intervention,

language-development support, and enrichment.

## Power and Confidence for the Information Age

Literacy Place uses technology as an integral part

of learning while connecting the classroom to the

real world.

3

# The Matrix

| PERSONAL LITERACY | INTELLECTUAL LITERACY | SOCIAL LITERACY |
|---|---|---|
| **Personal Voice** | **Problem Solving** | **Teamwork** |
| We communicate in our unique voices as we grow and learn. | People have the power to solve problems. | Successful teams depend on the collaboration of individuals. |

| **Stories About Us** | **See It, Solve It** | **All Together Now!** |
|---|---|---|
| **Big Idea** We listen to, tell, and create stories. | **Big Idea** We see problems and find solutions. | **Big Idea** We share and help each other. |
| **Mentor** Grandmother: *Honey Wada* | **Mentor** Clay Animator: *Becky Wible* | **Mentor** Pizza Maker: *Kwaku Twumasi* |
| **Place** Storytelling Corner | **Place** Claymator's Studio | **Place** Restaurant |
| **Project** "All About Me" Class Book | **Project** Dramatization | **Project** Big Book of Menus |

| **Hello!** | **Problem Patrol** | **Team Spirit** |
|---|---|---|
| **Big Idea** We share what we like. | **Big Idea** There are many kinds of problems. | **Big Idea** It's fun to do things together. |
| **Mentor** Author: *Donald Crews* | **Mentor** Veterinarian: *Fay Vittetoe* | **Mentor** Soccer Coach: *Danny Prenat* |
| **Place** Writer's Home | **Place** Veterinarian's Office | **Place** Soccer Stadium |
| **Project** Scrapbook | **Project** Pet Care Guide | **Project** Game Rule Book |

| **Snapshots** | **Super Solvers** | **Lights! Camera! Action!** |
|---|---|---|
| **Big Idea** Our actions tell about us. | **Big Idea** There may be more than one way to solve a problem. | **Big Idea** Creative teams produce great performances. |
| **Mentor** Photographer: *Bruce Thorson* | **Mentor** Toy Designer: *Mary Rodas* | **Mentor** Theater Director: *Judith Martin* |
| **Place** Sports Arena | **Place** Toy Company | **Place** Children's Theater |
| **Project** Exhibit | **Project** Safety Poster Campaign | **Project** Play Production |

| **What's New?** | **Big Plans** | **On the Job** |
|---|---|---|
| **Big Idea** We learn about our world through new experiences. | **Big Idea** Making and using plans can help us solve problems. | **Big Idea** Teams work best when they use each member's strengths to get the job done. |
| **Mentor** Wilderness Guide: *Keith Jardine* | **Mentor** Architect: *Jack Catlin* | **Mentor** Art Director: *Max Jerome* |
| **Place** Wilderness School | **Place** Construction Site | **Place** Ad Agency |
| **Project** Anecdote | **Project** Floor Plan | **Project** Ad Campaign |

| **Chapter by Chapter** | **What an Idea!** | **Discovery Teams** |
|---|---|---|
| **Big Idea** We are always adding to our life story. | **Big Idea** People solve problems by inventing new things. | **Big Idea** When we work as a team, we learn new things about our world. |
| **Mentor** Author: *Jerry Spinelli* | **Mentor** Inventor: *Julie Lewis* | **Mentor** Astronaut: *Dr. Mae Jemison* |
| **Place** Bookstore | **Place** Inventor's Office | **Place** Space Center |
| **Project** Personal Narrative | **Project** Invention Marketing Plan | **Project** Multimedia Presentation |

| **Making a Difference** | **It's a Mystery** | **Voyagers** |
|---|---|---|
| **Big Idea** Each of us is inspired by the lives of others. | **Big Idea** We can solve mysteries using reason, logic, and intuition. | **Big Idea** We depend on a network of people when we explore. |
| **Mentor** Musician: *Joseph Shabalala* | **Mentor** Forensic Chemist: *Lilly Gallman* | **Mentor** Travel Agent: *Marie French* |
| **Place** Concert Hall | **Place** Detective Headquarters | **Place** Travel Agency |
| **Project** Tribute | **Project** Investigative Report | **Project** Travel Magazine |

**scholastic.com**
Look for the Unit-by-Unit Extensions in the Literacy Place area.

| PERSONAL LITERACY | INTELLECTUAL LITERACY | SOCIAL LITERACY |
|---|---|---|
| **Creative Expression** | **Managing Information** | **Community Involvement** |
| People express themselves in many creative ways. | Finding and using information helps us live in our world. | Communities are built on the contributions of the people who live there. |

### Express Yourself

**Big Idea** We express ourselves through songs, sounds, stories, dance, and art.
**Mentor** Author: *Pat Mora*
**Place** Author's Studio
**Project** Storybook

### I Spy!

**Big Idea** Information is all around us.
**Mentor** Farmer: *Steven Powell*
**Place** Gardening Center
**Project** Garden Journal

### Join In!

**Big Idea** We help our community.
**Mentor** Singer/Songwriter: *Tom Chapin*
**Place** Performance Stage
**Project** Community Sing

### Imagine That!

**Big Idea** Imagination lets us look at things in new ways.
**Mentor** Muralist: *William Walsh*
**Place** Artist's Studio
**Project** Story Mural

### Information Finders

**Big Idea** Information comes from many sources.
**Mentor** Marine Biologist: *Laela Sayigh*
**Place** Aquarium
**Project** Big Book of Information

### Home Towns

**Big Idea** We are all members of a community.
**Mentor** Mayor: *Steve Yamashiro*
**Place** Mayor's Office
**Project** Visitor's Map

### Story Studio

**Big Idea** People express themselves through stories and pictures.
**Mentor** Author & Artist: *Tomie dePaola*
**Place** Author's Studio
**Project** Picture Book

### Animal World

**Big Idea** We use information to understand the interdependence of people and animals.
**Mentor** Zoo Curator: *Lisa Stevens*
**Place** Zoo
**Project** Zoo Brochure

### Lend a Hand

**Big Idea** People can make a difference in their communities.
**Mentor** Police Officer: *Nadine Jojola*
**Place** Police Station
**Project** Community Expo

### Hit Series

**Big Idea** A creative idea can grow into a series.
**Mentor** Author & Illustrator: *Joanna Cole & Bruce Degen*
**Place** Publishing Company
**Project** New Episode

### Time Detectives

**Big Idea** Finding information in stories and artifacts brings the past to life.
**Mentor** Archaeologist: *Dr. Ruben Mendoza*
**Place** Archaeological Site
**Project** Time Capsule

### Community Quilt

**Big Idea** In a community, some things continue and some things change.
**Mentor** Community Garden Director: *Lorka Muñoz*
**Place** Community Garden
**Project** Community Quilt

### The Funny Side

**Big Idea** Sometimes humor is the best way to communicate.
**Mentor** Cartoonist: *Robb Armstrong*
**Place** Cartoonist's Studio
**Project** Comic Strip

### Nature Guides

**Big Idea** Gathering and using information help us understand and describe the natural world.
**Mentor** Park Ranger: *Veronica Gonzales-Vest*
**Place** National Park Headquarters
**Project** Field Guide

### It Takes a Leader

**Big Idea** In every community there are people who inspire others to take action.
**Mentor** Editor: *Suki Cheong*
**Place** Newspaper Office
**Project** Op-Ed Page

### In the Spotlight

**Big Idea** We use our creativity to reach an audience.
**Mentor** Drama Coach: *José García*
**Place** Actor's Workshop
**Project** Stage Presentation

### America's Journal

**Big Idea** Considering different points of view gives us a fuller understanding of history.
**Mentor** Historian/Author: *Russell Freedman*
**Place** Historical Museum
**Project** Historical Account

### Cityscapes

**Big Idea** Cities depend on the strengths and skills of the people who live and work there.
**Mentor** Urban Planner: *Karen Heit*
**Place** Urban Planner's Office
**Project** Action Plan

# Components

## Pupil's Editions & Teacher's Editions

### Literacy Place Kindergarten

provides a rich learning environment including Big Books, Read Alouds, Sentence Strips, Audiocassettes, Phonics Manipulatives, Workbooks, Teacher Editions, and much more.

### Grades 1-5

▶ Literacy Place brings you what you would expect from Scholastic—authentic, award-winning children's literature.

▶ Our Teacher's Editions are easy to use, and provide explicit skills instruction.

▶ You'll also find a management CD-ROM to help you customize instruction to state and district standards.

**scholastic.com**
Check it out! You'll find a wealth of professional support resources, plus a lot of great stuff for kids and parents.

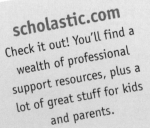

**Pupil's Editions**          **Teacher's Editions**

# Support Materials

## Practice
Literacy Place includes comprehensive practice resources.

- ✔ My Reading Workbook (1)
- ✔ Workshop and Project Cards (K-2)
- ✔ Practice Books (1-5)
- ✔ Spelling Resource Book (1-5)
- ✔ Grammar Resource Book (1-5)
- ✔ Handwriting Practice Book (K-3)
- ✔ ESL/ELD Resource Book (K-5)
- ✔ Skills Overhead Transparencies (2-5)
- ✔ Vocabulary Overhead Transparencies (2-5)
- ✔ Place Cards (3-5)

## Assessment
Literacy Place provides a wide range of assessment and evaluation options. (K-5)

- ✔ Placement Tests
- ✔ Assessment Handbook
- ✔ Classroom Management Forms
- ✔ Selection Tests (for every story!)
- ✔ Unit Tests (Forms A and B)
- ✔ Oral Reading Assessment
- ✔ Scholastic Reading Inventory
- ✔ TAAS Preparation and Practice Book
- ✔ Assessment System CD-ROM

## Technology
We set the industry standard.

- ✔ Phonics Practice CD-ROM (K-2)
- ✔ WiggleWorks Plus CD-ROM (K-2)
- ✔ Smart Place CD-ROM (3-5)
- ✔ Scholastic Management Suite (K-5)
- ✔ Staff Development Videos (K-5)
- ✔ Meet the Mentor Videos (K-5)
- ✔ Scholastic Network (K-5)
- ✔ Selection Audiocassettes (1-5)
- ✔ Classroom Resources CD-ROM (K-5)

## Scholastic Solutions
Only Scholastic can offer you the diverse range of materials you need for your classroom. Please call 1-800-Scholastic for a catalog. Ask about these exciting products:

- ✔ High-Frequency Readers (K-1)
- ✔ Sound and Letter Books (K-1)
- ✔ Big Books/Little Books (K-2)
- ✔ Phonemic Awareness Kit (K-2)
- ✔ Phonics Readers (K-3)
- ✔ Phonics Chapter Books (1-3)
- ✔ Phonics Workbooks (K-2)

- ✔ Guided Reading Program (K-5)
- ✔ Bilingual Support (K-5)
- ✔ Solares (K-5)
- ✔ Transition Program (3-6)
- ✔ Sprint Plus Intervention (3-6)
- ✔ READ 180 (4-8)
- ✔ Reading Counts! (K-8)

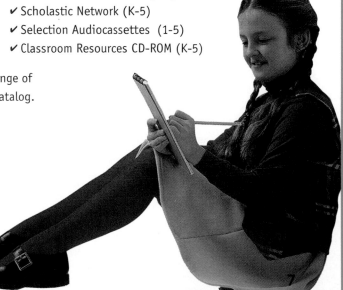

# Advisors

## Program Consultants

SKILLS, STRATEGIES, INSTRUCTION
**James Bauman**
*Professor, University of Georgia,*
Athens, Georgia

PHONICS AND EARLY READING
**Wiley Blevins**
*Consultant and Educational Writer*
New York, New York

ESL/ELD
**Jacqueline Kiraithe-Cordova**
*Professor, California State,* California

STAFF DEVELOPMENT
**Nancy Cummings**
*Western Director of Implementation*
*Success For All School Restructuring*
Phoenix, Arizona

BILINGUAL EDUCATION
**James Cummins**
*Professor, Ontario Institute for*
*Studies in Education*
Ontario, Canada

EARLY LITERACY DEVELOPMENT
**Nell K. Duke**
Michigan State University

ASSESSMENT/WRITING
**Adele Fiderer**
*Consultant and Educational Writer*
Scarsdale, New York

HANDWRITING
**Steve Graham**
*Professor, University of Maryland*
College Park, Maryland

WRITING
**Shelley Harwayne**
*Director of Manhattan New School*
New York, New York

SPELLING
**Richard E. Hodges**
*Professor, University of Puget Sound*
Tacoma, Washington

SPELLING
**Louisa Moats**
*County Office of Education*
Sacramento, California

VOCABULARY
**William E. Nagy**
*Assistant Professor, University of Illinois*
Champaign-Urbana, Illinois

FLEXIBLE GROUPING
**Michael Opitz**
*Professor, University of Colorado*
Boulder, Colorado

ESL/ELD
**Robert Parker**
*Consultant, Brown University*
Providence, Rhode Island

ESL/ELD
**Cao Anh Quan**
*ESOL Program Specialist*
Tallahassee, Florida

ESL/ELD
**Kim Quan Nguyen-Lam**
*California State University*
Long Beach, California

WRITING
**Michael Strickland**
*Author, Consultant*
Orange, New Jersey

## Teacher Reviewers

**Kim Andrews**
*Fourth Grade Reviewer*
Baltimore, Maryland

**Shirley Beard**
*Fourth Grade Reviewer*
El Paso, Texas

**Barbara Bloom**
*Fifth Grade Reviewer*
Wall Lake, Iowa

**Sherry Brown**
*Third Grade Reviewer*
Georgetown, Texas

**Lisa Buchholz**
*First Grade Reviewer*
Wheaton, Illinois

**Kathy Burdick**
*Fifth Grade Reviewer*
Austin, Texas

**Marianne Chorba**
*Fourth Grade Reviewer*
Baltimore, Maryland

**Peggy Colley**
*Third Grade Reviewer*
Rocky Face, Georgia

**Carol Curry**
*Third Grade Reviewer*
Tallahassee, Florida

**Claire Dale**
*First Grade Reviewer*
National City, California

**Mildred DeStefano**
*First Grade Reviewer*
Brooklyn, New York

**Doris Dillan**
*Grade Two Reviewer*
San Jose, California

**Oneaster Drummer**
*First Grade Reviewer*
Cincinnati, Ohio

**Ethel Durham**
*Third Grade Reviewer*
Grand Rapids, Michigan

**Patty Ernst**
*Second Grade Reviewer*
Naples, New York

**Alzada Fowler**
*First Grade Reviewer*
Lake Helen, Florida

**Jane Ginn**
*First Grade Reviewer*
Rohnert Park, California

**Amy Gordon**
*Third Grade Reviewer*
New City, New York

**Janet Gray**
*Fourth Grade Reviewer*
Lake Helen, Florida

**Velma Gunn**
*Fourth Grade Reviewer*
New Rochelle, New York

**Annie Ruth Harris**
*Third Grade Reviewer*
Decatur, Alabama

**Barbara Ann Hawkins**
*Second Grade Reviewer*
Hamer, South Carolina

**Amy Hom**
*Second Grade Reviewer*
New York, New York

**Min Hong**
*First Grade Reviewer*
Brooklyn, New York

**Susan Howe**
*Third Grade Reviewer*
Ellicott City, Maryland

**Barbara Jansz**
*First Grade Reviewer*
Naperville, Illinois

**Michele Jessen**
*First Grade Reviewer*
El Paso, Texas

**Ellen W. Johnson**
*Second Grade Reviewer*
Chalfont, Pennsylvania

**Vera Johnson**
*First Grade Reviewer*
Uniondale, New York

**Carol Kaiser**
*Third Grade Reviewer*
Los Angeles, California

**Karen Kolsky**
*Third Grade Reviewer*
Philadelphia, Pennsylvania

**Judy Keyak**
*Second Grade Reviewer*
St. Petersburg, Florida

**Jacqueline Krass**
*Second Grade Reviewer*
Gulfport, Mississippi

**Warren Livesley**
*Fourth Grade Reviewer*
New York, New York

**Libby Lesley**
*First Grade Reviewer*
San Angelo, Texas

**Dora I. Magana**
*Fourth Grade Reviewer*
El Paso, Texas

**Tim Mason**
*Second Grade Reviewer*
Willington Florida

**Carol Mercer**
*Fourth Grade Reviewer*
National City, California

**Betty Milburn**
*Third Grade Reviewer*
Grand Prairie, Texas

**Jane Moore**
*Third Grade Reviewer*
Dallas, Texas

**Sandy Nolan**
*Third Grade Reviewer*
Salem, Wisconsin

**Carol Ochs**
*Fifth Grade Reviewer*
Noble, Oklahoma

**Lynn Olson**
*Fifth Grade Reviewer*
Omaha, Nebraska

**Cynthia Orange**
*Second Grade Reviewer*
Bronx, New York

**Sue Panek**
*Fourth Grade Reviewer*
Hawthorne, New Jersey

**Deborah Peale**
*Fourth Grade Reviewer*
Miami, Florida

**Arturo Perez**
*Second Grade Reviewer*
Ventura, California

**Jeanette Reber**
*First Grade Reviewer*
Rock Hill, South Carolina

**Charlene Richardson**
*Fourth Grade Reviewer*
Everett, Washington

**Daria Rigney**
*Fifth Grade Reviewer*
Brooklyn, New York

**Andrea Ruff**
*First Grade Reviewer*
Brooklyn, New York

**Carol Shirmang**
*First Grade Reviewer*
Palatine, Illinois

**Wendy Smiley**
*Fourth Grade Reviewer*
Syracuse, New York

**Barbara Solomon**
*Second Grade Reviewer*
Hempstead, New York

**Alicia Sparkman**
*First Grade Reviewer*
Plant City, Florida

**Elaine Steinberg**
*Third Grade Reviewer*
Fresh Meadows, New York

**Bobby Stern**
*Third Grade Reviewer*
Winston-Salem, North Carolina

**Laura Stewart**
*First Grade Reviewer*

**Kate Taylor**
*Fifth Grade Reviewer*
Baltimore, Maryland

**Vasilika Terss**
*Second Grade Reviewer*
St. Louis, Missouri

**Linda Thorn**
*Fifth Grade Reviewer*
Cranford, New Jersey

**Gayle Thurn**
*Second Grade Reviewer*
Piedmont, South Carolina

**Jerry Trotter**
*Fifth Grade Reviewer*
Chicago, Illinois

**Julia Tucker**
*First Grade Reviewer*
Hampton, Virginia

**Patricia Viales**
*First Grade Reviewer*
Salinas, California

**Janielle Wagstaff**
*Second Grade Reviewer*
Salt Lake City, Utah

**Gail Weber**
*Fourth Grade Reviewer*
Sherman Oaks, California

**Elizabeth White**
*First Grade Reviewer*
Bronx, New York

**Karla Hawkins-Windeline**
*Second Grade Reviewer*
Hickman, Nebraska

## National Advisory Council

**Barbara R. Foorman, Ph. D.**
*Professor of Pediatrics*
*Director of the Center for*
*Academic and Reading Skills*
Houston, TX

**Dr. Wilmer Cody**
*Commissioner of Education*
*Kentucky State Department*
*of Education*
Frankfort, KY

**Ms. Judy Mountjoy**
*Vice President*
*The National PTA*
Chicago, IL

**Ms. Anne Bryant**
*Executive Director*
*National School Boards*
*Association*
Alexandria, VA

**Dr. Anthony Alvarado**
*Chancellor for Instruction*
*San Diego City Schools*
San Diego, CA

# TEACHER'S EDITION

SCHOLASTIC

# LITERACY PLACE®

UNIT 3

## All Together Now!

LITERACY PLACE AUTHORS

**CATHY COLLINS BLOCK**
Professor, Curriculum and Instruction, Texas Christian University

**LINDA B. GAMBRELL**
Professor, Education, University of Maryland at College Park

**VIRGINIA HAMILTON**
Children's Author; Winner of the Newbery Medal, the Coretta Scott King Award and the Laura Ingalls Wilder Lifetime Achievement Award

**DOUGLAS K. HARTMAN**
Associate Professor of Language and Literacy, University of Pittsburgh

**TED S. HASSELBRING**
Co-Director of the Learning Technology Center and Professor in the Department of Special Education at Peabody College, Vanderbilt University

**ADRIA KLEIN**
Professor, Reading and Teacher Education, California State University at San Bernardino

**HILDA MEDRANO**
Dean, College of Education, University of Texas-Pan American

**GAY SU PINNELL**
Professor, School of Teaching and Learning, College of Education, Ohio State University

**D. RAY REUTZEL**
Provost/Academic Vice President, Southern Utah University

**DAVID ROSE**
Founder and Executive Director of the Center for Applied Special Technology (CAST); Lecturer, Harvard University Graduate School of Education

**ALFREDO SCHIFINI**
Professor, School of Education, Division of Curriculum Instruction, California State University, Los Angeles

**DELORES STUBBLEFIELD SEAMSTER**
Principal, N.W. Harllee Elementary, Dallas, Texas; Consultant on Effective Programs for Urban Inner City Schools

**QUALITY QUINN SHARP**
Author and Teacher-Educator, Austin, Texas

**JOHN SHEFELBINE**
Professor, Language and Literacy Education, California State University at Sacramento

**GWENDOLYN Y. TURNER**
Associate Professor of Literacy Education, University of Missouri at St. Louis

Acknowledgments and credits appear on pages R28–R29, which constitute an extension of this copyright page.
Copyright © 2000 by Scholastic Inc.     All rights reserved.     Published by Scholastic Inc.     Printed in the U.S.A.

ISBN 0-439-07879-2 (National)

SCHOLASTIC, SCHOLASTIC LITERACY PLACE, and associated logos and designs are trademarks and/or registered trademarks of Scholastic Inc.

3  4  5  6  7  8  9  10          14          07  06  05  04  03  02  01  00

# TABLE OF CONTENTS

## All Together Now!

### We share and help each other.

## WEEKS 1 AND 2

# WEEKS 3 AND 4

# WEEKS 5 AND 6

# Kindergarten Place at a Glance

## PERSONAL VOICE
### Stories About Us
We listen to, tell, and create stories.

### WEEKS 1 AND 2
 **All I Am**
by Eileen Roe

**Chrysanthemum**
by Kevin Henkes

**Quick as a Cricket**
by Audrey Wood

WIGGLEWORKS PLUS: **Miss Mary Mack**

### WEEKS 3 AND 4
 **Coco Can't Wait!**
by Taro Gomi

**Pablo's Tree**
by Pat Mora

**Darlene**
by Eloise Greenfield

········ STORYTELLING ········
The Knee-High Man

### WEEKS 5 AND 6
 **I Like Books**
by Anthony Browne

**I Like Me!**
by Nancy Carlson

**The Little Red Hen**
by Paul Galdone

WIGGLEWORKS PLUS:
**What Lila Loves**

## PROBLEM SOLVING
### See It, Solve It
We see problems and find solutions.

### WEEKS 1 AND 2
 **What Am I?**
by N.N. Charles

**The Three Bears**
by Paul Galdone

**Where's My Teddy?**
by Jez Alborough

WIGGLEWORKS PLUS: **Birds on Stage**

### WEEKS 3 AND 4
 **I Went Walking**
by Sue Williams

**Caps for Sale**
by Esphyr Slobodkina

**Carlos and the Squash Plant**
by Jan Romero Stevens

WIGGLEWORKS PLUS: **Boots**

### WEEKS 5 AND 6
 **Is Your Mama a Llama?**
by Deborah Guarino

**Corduroy**
by Don Freeman

**Anansi the Spider: A Tale from the Ashanti**
by Gerald McDermott

········ STORYTELLING ········
The Three Billy Goats Gruff

## TEAMWORK
### All Together Now!
We share and help each other.

### WEEKS 1 AND 2
 **The 100th Day of School**
by Angela Shelf Medearis

**Herman the Helper**
by Robert Kraus

**The Cow That Went OINK**
by Bernard Most

WIGGLEWORKS PLUS: **Tortillas**

### WEEKS 3 AND 4
 **Jamberry**
by Bruce Degen

**Jamaica Tag-Along**
by Juanita Havill

**The Story of Chicken Licken**
by Jan Ormerod

········ STORYTELLING ········
The Great Big Enormous Turnip

### WEEKS 5 AND 6
 **Pizza Party!**
by Grace Maccarone

**Blueberries for Sal**
by Robert McCloskey

**Sione's Talo**
by Lino Nelisi

WIGGLEWORKS PLUS: **Pizza**

---

 **PHONOLOGICAL AWARENESS**

**ABC Song, Names, Alphabetic Knowledge**

**A Was Once an Apple Pie**
by Edward Lear

- **Mentor:** Honey Wada, a grandmother
- **Place:** Storytelling Corner

 **PHONOLOGICAL AWARENESS PHONICS**

**A B C D E F**

**Apples, Alligators and also Alphabets**
by Odette and Bruce Johnson

- **Mentor:** Becky Wible, a claymator
- **Place:** Claymator's Studio

 **PHONOLOGICAL AWARENESS PHONICS**

**G H I J K L**

**Eating the Alphabet: Fruits and Vegetables from A to Z**
by Lois Ehlert

- **Mentor:** Kwaku Twumasi, a pizza chef
- **Place:** Restaurant

## CREATIVE EXPRESSION
### Express Yourself
We express ourselves through songs, sounds, stories, dance, and art.

### WEEKS 1 AND 2
 **Listen to the Desert**
by Pat Mora

**A-Hunting We Will Go!**
by Steven Kellogg

**Mouse Mess**
by Linnea Riley

 WIGGLEWORKS PLUS:
**Let's Get the Rhythm**

### WEEKS 3 AND 4
 **The Itsy Bitsy Spider**
by Iza Trapani

**The Three Little Pigs**
by Gavin Bishop

**Mama Zooms**
by Jane Cowen-Fletcher

WIGGLEWORKS PLUS:
**Clifford the Big Red Dog**

### WEEKS 5 AND 6
 **Good-Night, Owl!**
by Pat Hutchins

**Minerva Louise at School**
by Janet Morgan Stoeke

**Whistle for Willie**
by Ezra Jack Keats

········ STORYTELLING ········
The Spider Weaver

## MANAGING INFORMATION
### I Spy!
Information is all around us.

### WEEKS 1 AND 2
 **Nature Spy**
by Shelley Rotner and Ken Kreisler

**Mice Squeak, We Speak**
by Tomie dePaola

**What Joe Saw**
by Anna Grossnickle Hines

········ STORYTELLING ········
The Coyote and the Turtle

### WEEKS 3 AND 4
 **From Head to Toe**
by Eric Carle

**Over on the Farm**
by Christopher Gunson

**Foal**
photographed by Gordon Clayton

 WIGGLEWORKS PLUS:
**A Tree Can Be...**

### WEEKS 5 AND 6
 **Flower Garden**
by Eve Bunting

**I Am the Peach**
by Luisa de Noriega

**The Tale of Peter Rabbit**
by Beatrix Potter

 WIGGLEWORKS PLUS: **My Garden**

## COMMUNITY INVOLVEMENT
### Join In!
We help our community.

### WEEKS 1 AND 2
 **My River**
by Shari Halpern

**Time to Sleep**
by Denise Fleming

**Rosie's Walk**
by Pat Hutchins

········ STORYTELLING ········
The Rabbit and the Elephant

### WEEKS 3 AND 4
 **What the Sun Sees, What the Moon Sees**
by Nancy Tafuri

**Abuela**
by Arthur Dorros

**The Little House**
by Virginia Lee Burton

 WIGGLEWORKS PLUS: **City Sounds**

### WEEKS 5 AND 6
 **Hattie and the Fox**
by Mem Fox

**Madeline's Rescue**
by Ludwig Bemelmans

**Officer Buckle and Gloria**
by Peggy Rathmann

 WIGGLEWORKS PLUS:
**Music Is in the Air**

---

**Phonics**

**PHONOLOGICAL AWARENESS PHONICS**

M N O P Q R -an, -op

**Alphabatics**
by Suse MacDonald

- **Mentor:** Pat Mora, an author
- **Place:** Author's Studio

**Phonics**

**PHONOLOGICAL AWARENESS PHONICS**

S T U V W X -at, -un, -ig

**Amazon Alphabet**
by Martin and Tanis Jordan

- **Mentor:** Steven Powell, a farmer
- **Place:** Gardening Center

**Phonics**

**PHONOLOGICAL AWARENESS PHONICS**

Y Z -en, -ot, CVC words

**ABCDrive!**
by Naomi Howland

- **Mentor:** Tom Chapin, a singer
- **Place:** Performance Stage

# RESTAURANT
# SETTING UP THE PLACE

## Why a Restaurant?

"Working in a restaurant involves working with other people. Only through teamwork can you get meals to customers."

*Kwaku Twumasi*

### Create a Workplace Model

Set up a restaurant in your classroom where children can experience teamwork and the importance of literacy in the workplace. Children can take on the roles of the different people who work at and use the restaurant.

### View the Mentor Video

View with children the video about people who work in a restaurant called Two Boots. Then talk with children about all of the people who worked in the restaurant.

**Recipe Chart**
Create a recipe chart in the kitchen for children to write and hang recipes on.

**Kitchen**
Set up a kitchen, with a sink, pizza oven, and work area.

- Provide measuring cups, spoons, bowls, pie tins, and other kitchen tools for children to use in their play. Play-dough can be used when children pretend to make pizza, bread, and other foods.

- Hang an order board in the kitchen for children to list customers' orders.

## Sign-in Chart

A restaurant workers' chart can be used for children to sign in as they play in the restaurant. Make columns for all of the jobs—cooks, dishwashers, busboys, and waiters—and ask children to sign their name in the appropriate column as they take on different roles.

## Menu

A chart billed "Today's Menu" can be displayed by the table so that customers can see what is available. Let children include daily specials and add new dishes regularly. Encourage children to include foods mentioned in the books they are reading.

## Waiters' Station

Set up a waiters' station where children can keep plates, cups, utensils, napkins, tablecloths, and other materials to set up the tables for customers.

- Include order pads and markers for the waiters to use in writing down customers' orders.

## Eating Area

A table and chairs for customers is an important part of the restaurant! Help children think of things they can add to the table to make it comfortable and friendly.

# WEEKS
# 1 AND 2

# Kindergarten Goals
## for Weeks 1 and 2

## Oral Language/ Vocabulary

- participating in group discussions
- building vocabulary for days and months; farm animals
- participating in choral reading
- discussing foods of different cultures
- exploring story vocabulary

## Reading

- building alphabetic knowledge
- participating actively in shared reading
- engaging in emergent reading
- making predictions
- exploring concepts of print
- sequencing story events
- using picture clues
- identifying action words
- chiming in on patterned text
- discussing problems and solutions
- reading high-frequency words

## Writing

- making a fruit and vegetable chart
- making a class schedule
- extending the story
- writing letters: *Gg, Hh*
- working with story pattern
- writing speech balloons
- engaging in shared writing
- writing independently in Journals

## Listening/Speaking/ Viewing

- listening to read alouds
- identifying rhyming words in stories
- listening to check predictions
- developing phonological awareness
- speaking in complete sentences
- dramatizing a story
- retelling a story
- singing songs
- connecting experiences with those of others
- sharing knowledge of other cultures
- demonstrating visual literacy

## Daily Phonics: *Gg* and *Hh*

- reciting classic poems, songs, and nursery rhymes
- naming and recognizing the letters
- recognizing sound/letter relationships
- generating words with /g/, /h/
- decoding words using /g/*g*, /h/*h*

## Center Workshops and Project

- acquiring world knowledge through cross-curricular activities
- creating a daily menu chart

# WEEKS 1 AND 2
# RESOURCES

## Big Book

### Meet the Author
Angela Shelf Medearis enjoys visiting children in schools because she doesn't remember authors visiting her schools when she was growing up.

### Meet the Illustrator
Joan Holub grew to love books by going to the library with her mother.

Available as audiocassette

## Big Book of Rhymes and Rhythms

For teaching phonological awareness, the alphabet, and concepts of print.

- "Old Mother Goose"
- "To Market"

Available as audiocassette

## Read Aloud

### Meet the Author
Robert Kraus sold his first cartoon at the age of ten. Eventually he decided to both write and illustrate children's books.

### Meet the Illustrators
José Aruego and Ariane Dewey create comic-looking animals to help tell their simple stories.

## Read Aloud

### Meet the Author/Illustrator
Bernard Most has been interested in art since he was four years old. He stresses the importance of "believing in yourself."

## ABC Book

### Meet the Author/Illustrator
Lois Ehlert, who lives in Milwaukee, Wisconsin, has always enjoyed artwork. She is known for dramatic color and shapes. When she creates a book she sometimes starts with the art, other times, the words!

**Side One**

**Side Two**

## SourceCard

- How can these children tell where everything belongs?
- "The Partner Dance"

## High-Frequency Reader

**My Read and Write Book**

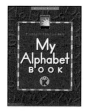

**My Alphabet Book**

**ESL/ELD Teaching Guide**

My Books

**To take home to share.**

# Introducing the Mentor

Kwaku Twumasi, the "pizza man" at Two Boots Restaurant, works with the line cook to coordinate the timing of the pizza orders. Piper, the manager/owner, rings up orders and makes change at the cash register. Together, they make the restaurant work!

# DAYS AT A GLANCE
## WEEKS 1 AND 2

| | Daily Phonics | Literature | Shared Writing | Workshops and Projects |
|---|---|---|---|---|
| **DAY 1** | Phonological Awareness: Oddity Task<br><br>Review /d/d, /e/e, /f/f | *Eating the Alphabet* by Lois Ehlert  | Make a Fruit and Vegetable Chart | Art: Fruit and Veggie Faces!<br><br>Math: Fruit and Vegetable Sort |
| **DAY 2** | **Consonant /g/g**<br>Phonological Awareness: Oral Segmentation | *The 100th Day of School* by Angela Shelf Medearis illustrated by Joan Holub | Make a Class Schedule | Art: What Can You Do With 100?<br><br>Math: All Sorts of Things |
| **DAY 3** | **Consonant /g/g**<br>Phonological Awareness: Alliteration<br><br>Introduce Sound-Spelling | *The 100th Day of School* by Angela Shelf Medearis<br>**High-Frequency Reader:** *Dogs* | Concepts of Print: Capital Letters<br><br>Write *Gg*<br><br>Make a Class Book | Math: How Many Blocks Tall?<br><br>Social Studies: Trash Graph |
| **DAY 4** | **Consonant /g/g**<br>Phonological Awareness: Oral Blending<br><br>Review Sound-Spelling | *Herman the Helper* by Robert Kraus illustrated by José Aruego & Ariane Dewey | Write a New Episode | Art: Animals of Clay<br><br>Science: Feed the Birds |
| **DAY 5** | **Consonant /g/g**<br>Phonological Awareness: Auditory Discrimination<br><br>Maintain Sound-Spelling | "Old Mother Goose" a rhyme<br>*Eating the Alphabet*<br>**My Book:** *In the Park* | Concepts of Print: Tracking Print<br><br>High-Frequency Word: *my* | Alphabet: *Gg*'s Galore<br><br>Health & Fitness: Gorillas and Geese! |

| | Daily Phonics | Literature | Shared Writing | Workshops and Projects |
|---|---|---|---|---|
| **DAY 6** | **Consonant /h/h**<br>Phonological Awareness: Oral Segmentation | *Tortillas*<br>by Margarita Gonzalez-Jensen | Innovate on the Text Pattern | Dramatic Play: "El Restaurante"<br><br>Cooking: Fill 'Er Up |
| **DAY 7** | **Consonant /h/h**<br>Phonological Awareness: Alliteration<br><br>Introduce Sound-Spelling | **SourceCard**<br>Where Does It Belong? "The Partner Dance"<br><br>**High-Frequency Reader:**<br>*Dogs* | Make a Classroom Helpers Chart<br><br>Write *Hh* | Writing: Classroom Improvement<br><br>Social Studies: Working Together Mural |
| **DAY 8** | **Consonant /h/h**<br>Phonological Awareness: Oral Blending<br><br>Review Sound-Spelling | *The Cow That Went OINK*<br>by Bernard Most | Write Animal Sound Speech Balloons | Cooking: Animal Crackers<br><br>Game: Animal Sound March |
| **DAY 9** | **Consonant /h/h**<br>Phonological Awareness: Oral Segmentation<br><br>Maintain Sound-Spelling | "To Market"<br>a rhyme<br><br>*Eating the Alphabet*<br>**My Book:** *We Clean Up* | Concepts of Print: Develop Print Awareness | Alphabet: A Heap of *Hh's!*<br><br>Dramatic Play: *Hh* Charades! |
| **DAY 10** | Phonological Awareness: Alliteration<br><br>Phonics Maintenance | **Review Books from Weeks 1 and 2** | Make a Compare and Contrast Chart | Project: Daily Menu |

**CHILDREN WILL:**

- identify words that begin with the same sound
- review /d/d, /e/e, /f/f
- read and respond to *Eating the Alphabet*
- build alphabetic knowledge
- participate in writing a group chart
- engage in Center Workshops

## MATERIALS

- *Apples, Alligators and also Alphabets*
- *Eating the Alphabet*
- Food magazines
- Sorting Cards

## GUIDED READING

To conclude each day's reading session, meet with guided reading groups. You might use Scholastic's Guided Reading Library or other books in your library.

# Share the ABC Book

## Warm-Up: Wordplay

### A PHONOLOGICAL AWARENESS

**Oddity Task** Gather the picture cards for *dog, duck, fan, fish,* and *fox*. Randomly display two of the cards at a time, and ask children to name the pictures. Then ask them to tell whether the beginning sounds are the same or different. Model an example.

**Think Aloud** d-d-dog, d-d-duck. *These words begin with the /d/ sound.* d-d-dog, f-f-fan. *These two words do not begin with the same sound.*

### B PHONICS MAINTENANCE

**/d/d, /e/e, /f/f** Invite children to chant the alphabet in order as you page through *Apples, Alligators and also Alphabets*. Stop briefly on the pages containing the letters *d, e,* and *f*. Ask children to say the sound that each letter stands for and to name what they see in the picture. Invite children to name other words that begin with each sound.

## Build Background

**ORAL LANGUAGE: FRUITS AND VEGETABLES**

Display the Fruit and Vegetable Sorting Cards.

▶ **Have you seen vegetables before they were picked?**

▶ **How are they different from those in the store?**

Then invite children to divide the Sorting Cards into two groups. Allow children to experiment with the characteristics that define each group (i.e. color, fruit, or vegetable).

**PREVIEW AND PREDICT**

Show the cover of *Eating the Alphabet*. Read the title and the author/illustrator's name, tracking the print.

▶ **Which fruits and vegetables are on the cover? Why do you think Lois Ehlert chose these?**

**SET A PURPOSE**

Ask children to tell what fruits and vegetables they think will be inside the book. Write down their ideas.

## Read the ABC Book

**ALPHABETIC KNOWLEDGE: *Gg* AND *Hh***

Read *Eating the Alphabet* from beginning to end with children. Invite them to say the letter names and the words for the fruits and vegetables on each page.

After you've read the book, review the pages for letters *Aa* through *Ff*. Then introduce the letters children will be learning about during the next two weeks—*Gg* and *Hh*.

**Eating the Alphabet**

## Respond to the Literature

**TALK ABOUT IT**

**Share Personal Responses** Invite children to respond to the book by sharing their favorite fruits and vegetables that were seen in the book. You may want to record their responses on a chart.

Encourage children to talk about the fruits and vegetables in the book that they had never heard of before.

▶ **Which new fruits and vegetables would you like to try?**

▶ **What do you think they might taste like?**

**THINK ABOUT IT**

**Focus on *Gg* and *Hh*** Turn to the page for *Gg* and *Hh*. Have children say the names of the fruits and vegetables they see. After they say each word, ask them to point to the beginning letter and to name it.

Invite children whose names begin with *Gg* or *Hh* to stand up. Help children to think of other words that begin with these sounds and letters. For example: *girl, gorilla; house, horse.*

**MODIFY Instruction**

**EXTRA HELP**

■ Bring in samples of the fruits and vegetables that won't be familiar to most children. Invite children to see, touch, smell, and taste these new foods. **(MULTISENSORY TECHNIQUES)**

## CULTURAL CONNECTION

Food is a tasty and colorful way to share different cultures. Encourage children to talk about their favorite foods. Do their families prepare special dishes for special days?

## MODIFY Instruction

### ESL/ELD

▲ Brainstorm the names of fruits and vegetables with children and list them in two columns on the board. Ask: *Which fruits are orange? Which vegetables are green? Which have skin? Which are sweet?* etc. Allow children to answer with single words or full sentences. **(CATEGORIZE)**

**MAKE A FRUIT AND VEGETABLE CHART**

# Shared Writing

Ask children to think about their favorite fruits and vegetables.

▶ **What do you like about your favorite fruit or vegetable?**

▶ **How do you like to eat it?**

Write **I like** _____ several times on a chart and invite each child to tell you his or her favorite fruit or vegetable. Fill in the sentences with children's responses. Invite children to supply the letters that they know.

Encourage children to illustrate the chart with pictures of the fruits and vegetables they named.

# Repeated Reading

**PREDICT LETTERS AND FOODS**

Reread the ABC book. Involve children in the reading by:

• guiding them to say the letter names along with you.

• encouraging them to name the pictures.

• asking them what they think the next alphabet letter will be and inviting them to predict what fruits and vegetables might be shown for that letter.

**READ AND WRITE INDEPENDENTLY**

**Journal** Place *Eating the Alphabet* in the Reading Center for children to read. Let children create and label pictures of fruits and vegetables in their Journals.

# ✔ Comprehension Check

**RETELL THE STORY**

Guide children to sit in a circle. Name a fruit or vegetable that begins with the letter *Aa* and invite the child next to you to name one that starts with *Bb*. Go around the circle, naming fruits and vegetables that begin with the letters *Aa* to *Zz*. Let children refer to the book for clues and possibilities when necessary.

**HOME/SCHOOL CONNECTION**

Give children the Family Newsletter from My Read and Write Book to bring home. Read the newsletter to children. Discuss what children will be doing in school and what they will say to their families.

# CENTER WORKSHOPS

## Art

### MATERIALS

- *Eating the Alphabet*
- Colored construction paper
- Large circle-shaped pieces of butcher paper or paper plates

## Fruit and Veggie Faces!

Show children the title page in *Eating the Alphabet*. Talk about how Lois Ehlert made a face with fruits and vegetables.

- Guide children to form small groups, and provide each group with a round piece of butcher paper or a paper plate. Invite children to draw pictures of fruits and vegetables or find pictures of them in supermarket flyers. Then ask children to cut out the pictures.
- Guide children to work together to decide how each fruit and vegetable can be part of a face. Invite children to glue the cutouts to the paper or plate to create faces.
- Display the fruit and vegetable faces for all to enjoy.

*Observation:* Notice which fruits and vegetables children draw or select. How do children decide which ones to use?

## Math

### MATERIALS

- Supermarket flyers
- Scissors
- Sorting Cards

## Fruit and Vegetable Sort

Provide supermarket flyers and other pictures of food. Encourage children to cut out pictures of fruits and vegetables to make sorting cards.

- Invite children to sort the pictures into two piles: *Fruits* and *Vegetables*.
- Talk about the fruits and vegetables, encouraging children to point out how they are similar and different.
- Ask children to name the different colors and shapes and to think of other ways they can sort the fruits and vegetables.

*Observation:* What similarities and differences do children point out among the fruits and vegetables?

## DAY 2 OBJECTIVES

**CHILDREN WILL:**

- listen for /g/
- name days and months
- read and respond to *The 100th Day of School*
- explore picture details
- write a class schedule
- engage in Center Workshops

## MATERIALS

- *The 100th Day of School*
- My Read and Write Book, pp. 5–6

The Big Book is available on audiocassette in the Literacy Place Listening Center.

The song is available on the **Sounds of Phonics** audiocassette.

# Share the Big Book

## DAILY PHONICS

## Consonant /g/g

### PHONOLOGICAL AWARENESS

**Oral Segmentation: Beginning Sounds** Sing or play the song, "Little Green Frog." Then say the word *gung* isolating the initial **/g/**: *g-g-gung*. Have children repeat the word isolating the initial **/g/**—g-g-gung.

- Invite children to join you during a second singing. Encourage them to exaggerate the initial **/g/** in *gung*.

### Little Green Frog

"Gung, gung," went the little green frog one day.
"Gung, gung," went the little green frog.
"Gung, gung," went the little green frog one day.
And his eye went "aah, aah, gung."

## Build Background

**ORAL LANGUAGE: DAYS AND MONTHS**

Point to the classroom calendar and ask children what day it is. Then ask them what month it is. Then ask:

▶ **On which day do we have gym class? On which days do we come to school?**

▶ **In which month is your birthday? What is the first month of the year?**

Invite children to join you as you name the days and months in order.

**PREVIEW AND PREDICT**

Show *The 100th Day of School*. Read the title and the names of the author and illustrator, tracking the print.

▶ **What do you think the children are doing?**

▶ **Why might the 100th day of school be special?**

## Read the Big Book

**NOTICE RHYME PATTERN**

As you read the book aloud, encourage children to notice what's happening in the pictures.

Children will begin to sense the rhythm of the lines and the rhyme pattern. Encourage them to use sound and picture clues to guess the rhyming word in every fourth line and to chime in when they feel comfortable.

## Respond to the Literature

**TALK ABOUT IT**

**Share Personal Responses** Invite children to talk about their reactions to the story.

▶ **What was your favorite part of the book?**

▶ **How would you celebrate the 100th day of school?**

▶ **How is the class in this story like your class? How is it different?**

**The 100th Day of School**

**THINK ABOUT IT**

**How We Celebrate** Invite children to share experiences they've had with celebrations.

▶ **What are some things you celebrate with friends, relatives, and neighbors?**

▶ **Why are celebrations important?**

▶ **If you could choose something to celebrate, what would it be? What kinds of things would you do to celebrate?**

### ESL/ELD

▲ Ask English language learners to name their favorite holiday or celebration. It can be from their country or the U.S. Have them answer questions: *Who do you celebrate with? What do you do on this day? Do you wear special clothes? Do you give and receive presents?* **(MAKE CONNECTIONS)**

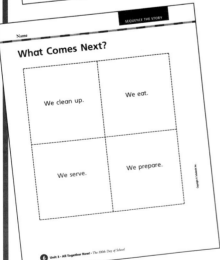

**My Read and Write Book, pp. 5–6**

## Shared Writing

**MAKE A CLASS SCHEDULE**

Invite children to brainstorm a list of activities they do as a class each day. Help them arrange their responses in the order they take place. Have children help you write the schedule on chart paper. You may want to include the time of day.

| Our Day | |
| --- | --- |
| 8:30 | Daily News |
| 9:00 | Reading / Writing |
| 10:00 | Recess |
| 10:30 | Snack |
| 10:45 | Storytime |

Read the schedule together, reviewing the time of day and activities. Invite children to illustrate the schedule with drawings, cutouts, and graphic designs. Post the schedule where children can refer to it.

**PUT A NOTE ON THE SCHEDULE**

Invite a volunteer to help write a note that says, "Our Day." Post the note next to the class schedule.

## Repeated Reading

**FOCUS ON SETTING**

Show children the cover of the Big Book and help them read the title. Tell children that although most of the story takes place in a classroom, some pages show the children in different settings.

As you reread the book, invite volunteers to point to the part of the pictures that give clues to the setting.

**READ AND WRITE INDEPENDENTLY**

**Journal** Place the audiocassette and copies of *The 100th Day of School* in the Reading Center so that children can read and listen to the book on their own or in small groups. Ask children to draw or write about favorite school activities in their Journals.

##  Comprehension Check

**ACT IT OUT**

Invite small groups to dramatize each activity or celebration as you read aloud the story.

# CENTER WORKSHOPS

## Math 123

### MATERIALS

- 100 pennies
- 100 blocks
- 100 unifix cubes

## What Can You Do with 100?

Invite children to work together in small groups to construct things with different materials. Children can:

- build a castle with 100 blocks.
- create a design or "drawing" with 100 pennies.
- connect 100 unifix cubes end to end.
- come up with their own ideas for using all 100 pieces of the material they choose.

*Observation:* How do the children work together to decide on and carry out a plan? How do they use the materials?

## Math 123

### MATERIALS

- Variety of classroom manipulatives and toys, including blocks, cubes, crayons, puzzles, and books
- Large boxes

## All "Sorts" of Things

At clean-up time, invite children to gather all the manipulatives and materials they have been using and place them in a pile in the center of the room.

- Let children work together to sort the materials into boxes.
- Encourage children to write a label for each box, such as "blocks," "crayons," and "books."
- When the sorting is complete, invite children to count the items in each box. Children may want to create picture graphs of their sorting and counting.

*Observation:* How are the children working together to make their sorting decisions?

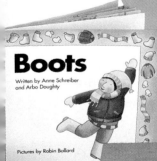

**Boots**

Written by Anne Schreiber and Arbo Doughty

Pictures by Robin Ballard

book

crayon

block

## DAY 3 OBJECTIVES

**CHILDREN WILL:**

- listen for alliteration
- recognize consonant /g/g
- write letter *Gg*
- reread *The 100th Day of School*
- recognize uppercase and lowercase letters
- explore picture details
- read High-Frequency Reader: *Dogs*
- identify the high-frequency word: *my*
- write a class book
- engage in Center Workshops

## MATERIALS

- *The 100th Day of School*
- High-Frequency Reader: *Dogs*
- My Alphabet Book, p. 9
- My Read and Write Book, p. 7

The Big Book is available on audiocassette in the Literacy Place Listening Center.

My Alphabet Book, p. 9

# Revisit the Big Book

and Read the High-Frequency Reader

**DAILY PHONICS**

## Consonant /g/g

### A PHONOLOGICAL AWARENESS

**Alliteration** Read aloud the following sentence.

*Gorillas and geese played a guessing game in the garden.*

Invite children to thump their chests like a gorilla when they hear the **/g/** sound. Have them repeat the sentence exaggerating the **/g/** sound.

### B CONNECT SOUND-SPELLING

**Introduce Consonant /g/g** Page through *Eating the Alphabet* until you get to the **Gg** page. Point out the letter **Gg** and explain that it stands for **/g/** as in **goose.**

- Ask children to say the sound with you.
- Say the names of the fruits and vegetables. Ask children to exaggerate the **/g/** at the beginning of each word.

## Letter Formation

**WRITE THE LETTER**

Write **Gg** on the chalkboard. Point out the uppercase and lowercase forms. Model how to write the letter using the rhymes provided.

- Have children write both forms of the letter in the air with their fingers. Ask children to make the letter's sound as they practice writing.

### G
Round the bowl, my guppies swim,
*(Circle left part way around.)*
Back and forth, rim to rim.
*(Pull left. Retrace. Pull right.)*

### g
There's a gopher in my garden,
See him going round.
*(Half-circle up and left.)*
Oops! Now the gopher sees me,
And he pops down in the ground!
*(Pull down. Curve up left.)*

## Reread the Big Book

**OPTIONS**

**Follow a Character** Help children identify the boy with glasses and locate him throughout the book. Ask them to tell what the boy is doing in each picture. How is he working and playing with classmates?

**Chime in on Rhyme** Before rereading the book, place sticky notes over the second rhyming word in each rhyming pair.

• Read the first three pages and guide children to name the first covered word: *day.*

• Point out that *play* and *day* rhyme because they end with the same sound: /ā/.

• As you continue to read, pause before the second rhyming word and let children predict it using listening clues and picture clues.

**The 100th Day of School**

**READ AND WRITE INDEPENDENTLY**

**Journal** Place copies of *The 100th Day of School* in the Reading Center for children to read alone or in small groups. Children can write in their Journals about their first day at school.

## Concepts of Print

**CAPITAL LETTERS**

Display the first page of the Big Book. Review the following concepts:

• a word is made up of letters.

• there are spaces between words.

• a sentence is made up of a group of words.

Then ask volunteers to look at a page and point out the beginning and end of a sentence. Guide children to notice that the first letter of the sentence is different from the others. Explain that the first word in a sentence always begins with a capital letter. Continue flipping through the book, inviting volunteers to point out the capital letters.

### GIFTED & TALENTED

✳ **Provide 100 pennies or counters. Encourage students to arrange them in equal-sized groups. Children may want to refer to specific pages of *The 100th Day of School* for ideas to get them started. How many ways can they group 100? (HANDS-ON LEARNING)**

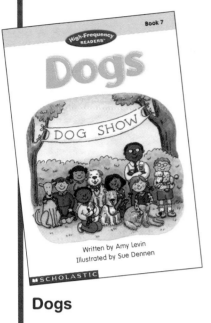

Written by Amy Levin
Illustrated by Sue Dennen

**SCHOLASTIC**

**Dogs**

**TEACHER TIP**

Take notice of how children grip their pencils, position their papers, and begin to form letters as they write.

**My Read and Write Book, p. 7**

## Read High-Frequency Reader

**INTRODUCE THE BOOK**

Show the book *Dogs*. Read the title and the author's name. Explain that the book is about a dog show.

▶ **Do you have a dog or another pet? What is your pet's name?**

▶ **What tricks can your pet do?**

**HIGH-FREQUENCY WORD: *my***

On the board, write the sentence stem *My dog can _____.* Read it aloud. Underline the word ***My.*** Then write the word ***my*** on a note card. Read it aloud.

• Display the card and have children read the word.

• Help children spell it aloud, clapping on each letter.

• Ask children to write it in the air as they state aloud each letter.

Review the high-frequency word ***can.*** Help children read the story word ***dog.*** Invite volunteers to suggest words to complete the sentence. Write each new sentence on the board.

Add the card for ***my*** to the Word Wall.

**SHARE THE HIGH-FREQUENCY READER**

Read the story aloud, tracking the print. Invite children to point to the high-frequency word ***my.***

• After each page, ask children if they know a dog or other animal who can do the same trick.

**SHARED WRITING**

Invite children to make a class book called *My Pet*.

• Ask each child to think of a trick that a pet can do. Help children write and complete the sentence *My pet can _____.* Encourage them to illustrate their sentences. Bind the pages into a book and share it with the class.

# CENTER WORKSHOPS

**Math 123**

## How Many Blocks Tall?

Children can find out how many blocks tall they are. One child can lie on the floor as a partner lays same-size blocks end to end next to him or her. Have them begin at the bottom of the feet and measure to the top of the head.

### MATERIALS
- Wooden blocks
- Chart paper
- Markers
- Sticky notes

- List children's names on a chart. Help children count how many blocks tall they are and to record their measurements next to their names.

- Children might use one sticky note for each block used to make one-to-one correspondences.

*Observation:* Notice how children work together and how they count the blocks.

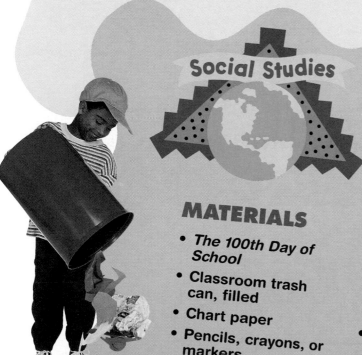

**Social Studies**

## Trash Graph

Review how the children in *The 100th Day of School* recycled cans and newspapers. Briefly discuss the importance of recycling. Then talk about the kinds of garbage that the class throws away each day.

### MATERIALS
- *The 100th Day of School*
- Classroom trash can, filled
- Chart paper
- Pencils, crayons, or markers

- For a week, children can collect trash materials such as paper, juice cups, and broken supplies in separate boxes. Then small groups can take turns counting how many of each item are thrown out each day. Each group can draw pictures on a class graph to represent the trash they find.

- Discuss ways to reduce classroom waste.

*Observation:* How do children use their discoveries to help them problem-solve?

## DAY 4 OBJECTIVES

**CHILDREN WILL:**

- orally blend onset and rime
- review consonant /g/g
- talk about being helpers
- read and respond to *Herman the Helper*
- write a new episode
- explore sequence
- engage in Center Workshops

## MATERIALS

- *Herman the Helper*
- *My Read and Write Book,* p. 8

## TECHNOLOGY

 Children can think of made-up names for some of the animals in this story. Encourage them to use the **WiggleWorks Plus** Magnet Board to combine and modify animal names they already know. Invite them to add illustrations.

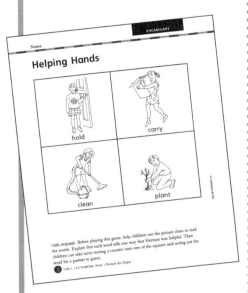

VOCABULARY

Name

Helping Hands

hold / carry / clean / plant

Oral Language: Before playing this game, help children use the picture clues to read the words. Explain that each word tells one way that Herman was helpful. Then children can take turns tossing a counter onto one of the squares and acting out the word for a partner to guess.

Unit 1 • A-3 Together Time • *Herman the Helper*

**My Read and Write Book, p. 8**

# Share the Read Aloud

### DAILY PHONICS

## Consonant /g/g

**Ⓐ PHONOLOGICAL AWARENESS**

**Oral Blending** Read the following word parts aloud and ask children to blend them. Provide corrective feedback and modeling when necessary.

| | | |
|---|---|---|
| /g/. . . ame | /g/. . . irl | /g/. . . oat |
| /g/. . . ift | /g/. . . ate | /g/. . . ood |

**Ⓑ CONNECT SOUND-SPELLING**

**Make a Gift Box** Draw a large gift box on a piece of chart paper. Write the word *gift* and circle the letter **g.** Remind children that the letter **g** stands for **/g/.**

Invite children to think of other words that begin with **/g/** to put in the gift box. List their responses. Invite volunteers to circle the **g** at the beginning of each word. Children can illustrate some of their "gift" words.

## Build Background

**ORAL LANGUAGE: BEING HELPFUL**

Ask children what they think it means to be helpful.

▶ **Who have you helped? How did you help?**

▶ **How does it make you feel when you help someone?**

▶ **How has someone helped you?**

**PREVIEW AND PREDICT**

Show the cover of *Herman the Helper.* Read the title and the author's and illustrators' names, tracking the print.

▶ **Do you think Herman is shown in this illustration? Which character do you think he is? Why?**

**SET A PURPOSE**

Invite children to suggest helpful things Herman will do. Have them listen to find out if their predictions are correct.

## Share the Read Aloud

**FOCUS ON PROBLEMS AND SOLUTIONS**

As you read aloud the story, change your voice to reflect the difference between the narration at the top of each page and the characters' dialogue which appears in smaller print.

- After each page, give children an opportunity to study the illustrations. Ask what problem each animal has and how Herman helps them.

- When you get to the next-to-last page, where Herman's father offers to help him to mash potatoes, invite children to predict what they think Herman might say.

**Herman the Helper**

## Respond to the Literature

**TALK ABOUT IT**

**Share Personal Responses** Invite children to share ideas and questions about the story. To encourage sharing, ask questions such as the following:

▶ Why did the animals call Herman when they needed help?

▶ Who do you think Herman helped the most?

▶ Do you think Herman enjoyed helping others? Why or why not?

▶ How did the other animals thank Herman?

**THINK ABOUT IT**

**Discuss Helpfulness** Use the story to explore the concept of helpfulness.

▶ What are some ways that the other animals might help Herman?

▶ What are some ways we help each other at school?

▶ Why is helping important?

▶ Why is saying "thank-you" important?

### MODIFY Instruction

#### EXTRA HELP

■ Invite small groups of children to act out some of the ways that Herman helped his friends and family. **(ACT IT OUT)**

**MODIFY**
Instruction

## EXTRA HELP

■ To provide extra practice with the concept of sequence, show three pictures of a simple activity being carried out. For example, someone eating dinner, finishing dinner, and clearing the table. Invite children to place the pictures in the proper sequence to tell the "story." **(SEQUENCE)**

## Shared Writing

**WRITE A NEW EPISODE**

Ask children to recall ways that Herman helped other animals in the story.

▶ **Who did Herman help?**

▶ **Did Herman ever say no to anyone in trouble?**

▶ **What should you say after someone has helped you?**

Write *thank you* on the chalkboard.

Invite children to extend the story by thinking of one more animal Herman could help.

▶ **What animal is in trouble?**

▶ **How can Herman help?**

List ideas on the board. Then encourage children to create a new page for the book by drawing a picture of Herman helping someone else. Help children label their pictures with *Thank-you, Herman.*

## Repeated Reading

**EXPLORE STORY SEQUENCE**

As you reread the story, focus on how the pictures illustrate the sequence of events that show how Herman was helpful. Pause after reading the page where Herman helped his father.

▶ **What is the difference between the first picture and the second picture? the second and third pictures?**

▶ **Would it make sense if the illustrator showed the third picture first? Why?**

Guide children to understand that when story events are in the correct order, or sequence, it helps readers understand what is happening.

**READ AND WRITE INDEPENDENTLY**

**Journal** Place *Herman the Helper* in the Reading Center so children can read it independently. Children may want to write in their Journals about friends they have helped.

##  Comprehension Check

**RETELL THE STORY**

Invite volunteers to retell the story as you show the pictures. On each page encourage children to tell how Herman is helping.

# CENTER WORKSHOPS

**Art**

## Animals of Clay

Ask children to look for the animals on each page of *Herman the Helper*. How many different animals do they spot? Children can make a list of the animals in the book.

- Invite children to choose animals from the list to model from clay.

- Encourage a small group of children to paint a mural of the ocean habitat to display behind the clay animals. Children can write the names of their animals on small pieces of paper and tape them to the ocean mural.

*Observation:* Notice how children refer to the book for information as they make the animal models and paint the mural.

### MATERIALS

- **Herman the Helper**
- **Clay**
- **Mural paper**
- **Paint and brushes**
- **Pencils or markers**
- **Paper**
- **Tape**

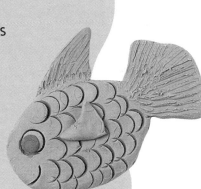

**Science**

## Feed the Birds

Discuss how children can help animals just like Herman did. Children can make bird feeders by spreading peanut butter over pine cones. Pour bird seed into the pan, and let children roll the peanut-butter pine cones in the bird seed. Tie a string to the top of the pine cones and place the feeders in bags for children to take home.

After a few days, talk about where children placed their bird feeders and how it made them feel to help the birds.

*Observation:* How do children go about building a bird feeder? What connection do they make between their project and being helpers?

### MATERIALS

- **Pine cones**
- **Peanut butter**
- **Craft sticks**
- **String**
- **Bird seed**
- **Large flat pan with sides**
- **Paper bags**

**CHILDREN WILL:**

- listen for /g/
- read a rhyme
- recognize sound spelling relationships for /g/g
- review high-frequency words
- read My Book: *In the Park*
- engage in Center Workshops

## MATERIALS

- *Big Book of Rhymes and Rhythms*, p. 12
- Sentence Strips for "Old Mother Goose"
- *Eating the Alphabet*
- My Read and Write Book, p. 9
- My Book: *In the Park*

**My Read and Write Book, p. 9**

For additional practice see *Scholastic Phonics K,* pp. 39–42. See also Sound and Letter book: *Let's Go.*

# Sounds and Letters

**DAILY PHONICS**

and Read My Book

# Consonant /g/g

## Ⓐ PHONOLOGICAL AWARENESS

**Auditory Discrimination** Remind children they are learning about the sounds of language and the letters that stand for those sounds. Read aloud "Old Mother Goose" from the *Big Book of Rhymes and Rhythms*. As you come to words that start with **/g/**, emphasize the initial sound. Repeat the rhyme a few times, encouraging children to chime in. Have them honk like a goose after every **/g/** sound they hear.

**Big Book of Rhymes and Rhythms, p. 12**

## Ⓑ CONCEPTS OF PRINT

Put the *Big Book of Rhymes and Rhythms,* the Sentence Strips for "Old Mother Goose," and a pocket chart in the Reading Center. Then do the following:

- Read the rhyme together, letting children pretend to fly on a gander as they recite the rhyme.

- Read the rhyme again, one line at a time. Ask a volunteer to find the Sentence Strip that shows the line and place it in the pocket chart.

- When the whole rhyme is assembled, invite children to read it again, having volunteers help you track the print on each line.

- Invite children to find the words that begin with **Gg.** Read them together.

Old Mother Goose,

When she wanted to wander,

Would ride through the air

On a very fine gander.

**PROFESSIONAL DEVELOPMENT**

**DAVID ROSE**

*How Can Technology Help?*

 *Technology offers another avenue through which literacy instruction can occur. Using **WiggleWorks Plus**, children can read text with the degree of support necessary by clicking on the words, phrases, or sentences that pose difficulty. In addition, the Magnet Board offers opportunities for both structured and unstructured wordplay to reinforce knowledge of phonics and high-frequency words.*

Ⓒ **CONNECT SOUND-SPELLING**

**Alphabetic Principle** Remind children that the letter *g* stands for **/g/** as in *goose*. Page through *Eating the Alphabet* as children chant the letters. Briefly review the sound that each letter stands for, stopping on the letter *Gg*. Show the ABC Card for *Gg*, if available. Invite children to name the picture and letter.

**ABC Book** Invite children to make a new page for their ABC book. Ask children to name animals, foods, people, and objects whose names begin with **/g/**. When the list is complete, encourage children to work together to create the *Gg* page for the ABC Book.

**Goose, Goose, Duck** Invite children to play Goose, Goose, Duck using word cards. Prepare enough word cards for each child in the class. Write *Goose* on all of them except for one. This card will say *Duck*. Help children read the cards. The game will proceed like Duck, Duck, Goose except that the child who is "it" will hand out the word cards instead of saying *duck* or *goose*.

Ⓓ **VOCABULARY: HIGH-FREQUENCY WORDS**

Write the sentence *I see my book* on the chalkboard and read it aloud.

• Put the word cards for *I, see*, and *my* in a pocket chart. Review each word using the read-spell-write approach.

• Write *book* on a card and put it in the pocket chart. Invite a volunteer to read the sentence.

• Invite children to look at something that belongs to them. Have them describe it so that their classmates can guess the object.

• Write the word on a card and cover the previous word. Ask children to explain how the meaning of the sentence changes when one word is changed.

**TECHNOLOGY**

Children can write the words pictured here on the **WiggleWorks Plus** Magnet Board. Explode words to mix up the letters. Then invite children to rewrite the words.

The rhyme in the *Big Book of Rhymes and Rhythms* is available on the **Sounds of Phonics** audiocassette.

**In the Park**

## MODIFY Instruction

### ESL/ELD

▲ **English language learners may benefit from pantomiming the activities they read about in *In the Park*. Have more fluent speakers look at the pictures and describe what they see. Ask: *Do you like to play ball?* (PANTOMIME)**

# Read My Book

**INTRODUCE THE BOOK**

Let children know that they are going to get their own book that they can read on their own and take home.

▶ **What games do you play in groups?**

▶ **What are some things you do together outside?**

**PREVIEW AND PREDICT**

Pass out copies of *In the Park*. Read the title and the author's and illustrator's names.

▶ **Where do you think these kids might be?**

▶ **What do you think this book might be about?**

**READ TOGETHER**

Read the My Book with children, tracking the print as you read. Guide children to read along in their copies, and to discuss what the different children are doing.

**PHONICS**

Ask children to say the word *build* aloud.

▶ **What sound do you hear at the beginning of the word? What letter stands for that sound?**

Invite children to find the word *build* in their My Books. Continue with other letters children have learned.

**READ AND WRITE INDEPENDENTLY**

**Journal** Encourage children to read *In the Park* on their own or in small groups. Provide crayons and invite children to color the illustrations. Have them write in their Journals about their favorite park activities.

**HOME/SCHOOL CONNECTION**

Children can take home their My Books to share with family members and friends. Suggest that children make books about the things they do in their park or yard.

# CENTER WORKSHOPS

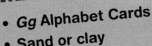

## Gg's Galore

Invite children to make *Gg* using different kinds of materials. Using the Alphabet Cards as a model, children can:

- trace *Gg* in the sand.
- form the letters with ropes of clay or colored glue.
- draw the letters with finger paints.

The choice is theirs!

*Observation:* How do children choose to form *Gg*'s?

### MATERIALS
- **Gg Alphabet Cards**
- **Sand or clay**
- **Trays**
- **Finger paints**
- **Oaktag paper**
- **Colored glue**

## Gorillas and Geese!

Invite children to imitate animals with *Gg* names. One child can choose an animal card and move and make noises like that animal. The rest of the children can guess the animal.

Then use the animal cards a different way. Play some music that is good background sound for making animal movements. One child can be a "Caller." The child can hold up an animal card and say the animal's name. Everyone must move like that animal. When the Caller holds up a different card and says a different name, children move like the new animal.

*Observation:* How do children act like the animals?

### MATERIALS
- **Labeled pictures of animals with *Gg* names (goose, gorilla, goat, gopher, grasshopper, grizzly bear, gull)**

# Share the WiggleWorks Book

## DAY 6 OBJECTIVES

**CHILDREN WILL:**

- orally segment words (beginning sounds)
- listen for /h/
- talk about families and cultures
- speak in complete sentences
- innovate on the text pattern
- engage in Center Workshops

## MATERIALS

- *Tortillas*
- **My Read and Write Book,** p. 10

## GUIDED READING

To conclude each day's reading session, meet with guided reading groups. You might use Scholastic's Guided Reading Library or other books in your library.

## TECHNOLOGY

 Children can interact with the **WiggleWorks Plus** selection on the computer. Encourage them to use the **WiggleWorks Plus** tools to read the story and click on words to hear them read aloud. Ask children to use the Record tool to record themselves saying the same words.

 The song is available on the **Sounds of Phonics** audiocassette.

### DAILY PHONICS

## Consonant /h/h

### PHONOLOGICAL AWARENESS

**Oral Segmentation: Beginning Sounds** Sing or play the song, "The Hokey Pokey." Lead children in doing the actions. After the first verse, say the words *h-h-hokey* and *h-h-hand*, isolating the initial **/h/.** Have children say the words as you do. Invite them to continue the song using **/h/** words such as *hip, head,* and *hair.* Encourage them to think of other parts of the body and to say the initial sound.

#### The Hokey Pokey

1. **You put your right hand in,
   You put your right hand out.
   You put your right hand in,
   And you shake it all about.
   You do the Hokey Pokey,
   And you turn yourself around.
   That's what it's all about.**
2. **You put your left hand in . . .**

## Build Background

**ORAL LANGUAGE: SHARE CULTURAL BACKGROUNDS**

Invite children to share what they know about tortillas. What is a tortilla? Where have children had tortillas? Begin a discussion about breads from around the world. Invite children to talk about special breads they eat with their families. Guide children to speak in complete sentences.

**PREVIEW AND PREDICT**

Show the book and read the title and the author's and illustrator's names. Ask children to predict what this story is about.

## Read the WiggleWorks Book

**EXPLORE STORY VOCABULARY**

Encourage children to note the different ways characters in the book eat tortillas. Which toppings would children like to try?

Encourage children to identify the words on each page that describe the tortillas and how they are eaten. Emphasize that words such as *crisp* and *soft* are descriptive words. Ask children to compare how crisp and soft tortillas would look, taste, feel, and sound when eaten.

**Tortillas**

## Respond to the Literature

**TALK ABOUT IT**

**Share Personal Responses** Ask children if they liked the story.

▶ **Did reading the story make you hungry?**

▶ **How did the people in the story like to eat tortillas?**

▶ **How would you like to eat tortillas?**

▶ **Why do you think the author wrote about tortillas?**

▶ **Does your family eat tortillas? What other foods from other countries do you like to eat?**

**THINK ABOUT IT**

**Helping at Mealtime** Guide children in noticing that many of the illustrations show family members in the kitchen together. Lead a discussion of cooking, eating, and cleaning up in children's homes.

▶ **How is teamwork a part of mealtime?**

▶ **What jobs can you do to help?**

### MODIFY Instruction

#### ESL/ELD

▲ If there are children in your class who eat tortillas at home, ask them to bring some in to share with the class. They can contribute a lot to a discussion on ingredients, how to make tortillas, or food that you can put in tortillas. **(MAKE CONNECTIONS)**

### TECHNOLOGY

Ask children to read the story on **WiggleWorks Plus** and find pairs of words that are opposites. Children can add them to their My Words list: *big/little, soft/crisp.* Then encourage children to find other words in the story that have opposites like *hot (cold)* or *off (on).*

## TECHNOLOGY

Let children use an art program to draw a tortilla topped with things they think would taste good. When they have created their perfect tortilla, encourage them to write a description of it, or recipe for it.

**My Read and Write Book, p. 10**

## Shared Writing

**INNOVATE ON THE TEXT PATTERN**

Ask children to think about a food they eat often in their households. As a group, decide which food to write about. Work together to write a story that follows the pattern of *Tortillas*. You might use the example below to get children started. Guide children to write from left to right and from top to bottom.

> Bread, Bread.
> We eat it plain.
> We eat it covered with jam.
> Bread, bread.
> We eat it with butter,
> hot from the toaster.

## Repeated Reading

**CHIME IN ON THE STORY PATTERN**

Knowing the pattern of *Tortillas* will help children to read the text. The repeated line "Tortillas, tortillas" is followed by "We eat . . ." and one or two ways to eat tortillas.

Point out the word *Tortillas* on the cover before you reread the story. As you go through the book, encourage children to point out the word *tortillas* each time it appears in the text. Invite them to chime in on the repeated phrases.

**READ AND WRITE INDEPENDENTLY**

**Journal** Place the book in the classroom library so children can enjoy *Tortillas* on their own or with a friend. They can draw or write in their Journals about experiences with tortillas.

## ✅ Comprehension Check

**ACT IT OUT**

Invite children to create a sound or action to accompany each line of the text as you narrate the story.

# CENTER WORKSHOPS

## Dramatic Play

## El Restaurante

Provide props and costumes and invite children to create a Mexican restaurant in the Dramatic Play Center. Encourage children to use teamwork and decide together who will role-play as servers, cooks, customers, and strolling musicians. Encourage children who have watched tortillas being made to demonstrate the process for other children.

Add culturally appropriate music to complete the atmosphere. Encourage customers to order food the way they like it and invite servers to take orders by asking questions about the customers' preferences.

*Observation:* Notice how children use writing to take orders.

### MATERIALS

- Kitchen props
- Sample menus from a Mexican restaurant
- Modeling clay
- Maracas and claves
- Audiocassette of Mexican music

## Cooking

## Fill 'Er Up

Invite children to work in pairs to make a tortilla filling. Children can decide together how to fill, roll, and eat their tortillas.

Encourage children to write a picture recipe for their tortilla roll-up and to create a name for it. Guide children to talk about how they had fun planning, cooking, writing, eating, and cleaning up as a team.

*Observation:* How do children work together as they prepare their tortillas?

### MATERIALS

- Small, soft tortillas
- Variety of fillings, which might include tomatoes, salsa, cheese, beans, guacamole, and sour cream
- Paper plates
- Napkins

## DAY 7 OBJECTIVES

**CHILDREN WILL:**

- listen for alliteration
- recognize /h/h and write *Hh*
- demonstrate visual literacy
- sing a song
- write a classroom helpers chart
- read High-Frequency Reader: *Dogs*
- engage in Center Workshops

## MATERIALS

- *Teamwork*, SourceCard 1
- High-Frequency Reader: *Dogs*
- My Alphabet Book, p. 10

## TECHNOLOGY

 Encourage children to use the drawing and writing tools in the **WiggleWorks Plus** Write area to complete the activities.

My Alphabet Book, p. 10

# Read the SourceCard

 **DAILY PHONICS**

 and Read the High-Frequency Reader

## Consonant /h/h

### Ⓐ PHONOLOGICAL AWARENESS

**Alliteration** Say the following sentence aloud, emphasizing the initial **/h/** in most of the words.

*Hippos wear heavy helmets to play hockey.*

Invite children to repeat the sentence emphasizing the initial **/h/.**

### Ⓑ CONNECT SOUND-SPELLING

**Introduce Consonant /h/h** Page through *Eating the Alphabet* until you get to the **Hh** page. Point out that the letter **Hh** stands for **/h/** as in **huckleberry.**

- Ask children to say the sound with you.
- Help children to think of other **/h/** words such as *hat, hand,* or *horse* by giving clues. Write these words on the board and have children point to the letter **Hh.**

## Letter Formation

**WRITE THE LETTER**

Write **Hh** on the chalkboard. Point out the uppercase and lowercase forms. Model how to write the letter using the rhymes below.

- Have children write both forms of the letter in the air with their fingers. Ask children to make the letter's sound as they practice writing. Note their paper position, pencil grip, and beginning stroke.

| H | h |
|---|---|
| **Go down and down. Make two big poles.** *(Pull down straight, twice.)* **Across in the middle like a post for goals.** *(Pull straight across.)* | **Fall a long way down, bounce back with a bump.** *(Pull down straight, retrace halfway up.)* **Around and down to make a hump.** *(Go over and down.)* |

## Share the SourceCard

**SIDE ONE**

**How We Help Each Other** Guide children to look at the photograph of children working together to clean up the classroom. Read the question "How can these children tell where everything belongs?"

Invite children to point out an item that still needs to be put away.

▶ **How can you tell where it belongs?**

▶ **Do the labels help you decide where each item goes?**

Talk about the labels in the photograph and what they tell us. How do children know where things go in their own classroom? Talk about why people put things away in the same place.

**SIDE TWO**

**Share the Folk Song** Read the lines to *The Partner Dance,* emphasizing the rhyme at the end of each line. Invite children to sing the lines of the song with you. Check to see if children can find their left and right arms before they stand up and face a partner. Practice singing, then dance through the motions of the song.

Side One

How can these children tell where everything belongs?

Side Two

The Partner Dance
Partner, come and dance with me,
Both my hands I give to thee,
Right foot first, left foot then,
Turn a-round and back a-gain.
With my feet I tap, tap, tap,
With my hands I clap, clap, clap,
Right foot first, left foot then,
Turn a-round and back a-gain.

German folk song from *Hansel and Gretel*

## Shared Writing

**MAKE A CLASSROOM HELPERS CHART**

Ask children what they like to do to help clean up the classroom. Chart each child's responses.

Help children create a "Classroom Helpers" chart by attaching children's name cards to a Bulletin Board. Then on another card help them write the name of a job each will do in the coming week. Invite them to illustrate the jobs. You may want to update this chart each week by moving the job cards.

**MODIFY Instruction**

### ESL/ELD

▲ Help English language learners express their ideas for the chart by first pantomiming different cleaning actions while you supply the word for the action, for example: *clean, pick up, order, wash,* and *paint.* List the words on the chalkboard and read them with children. **(USE LISTS)**

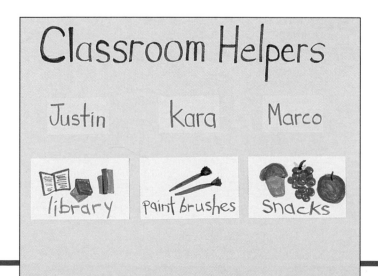

Classroom Helpers

Justin     Kara     Marco

library     Paint brushes     Snacks

**Dogs**

## PROFESSIONAL DEVELOPMENT

**JOHN
SHEFELBINE**

*Why Focus on High-Frequency
Words?*

*Directly teaching high-
frequency words is
important because (a) a
relatively small number of
words occur very often and
knowing them can be very
advantageous to the beginning
reader, (b) at least 15% of
high-frequency words cannot
be easily sounded out because
they are irregular, and (c) even
some regular high-frequency
words need to be taught
because beginning readers may
not know enough sound-
spellings to sound them out.*

## Revisit High-Frequency Reader

**REREAD
THE BOOK**

Invite children to join you as you read *Dogs* again. On the
first page, have children read and review the two words
that they have already learned (*My* and *can*).

**DECODING
STRATEGIES**

As you go through the book, point to each word, the
picture clue, the initial letter and any other sound-
spellings children have learned. Pause long enough for
children to read the words before you do. Model blending
as needed. For example, have children use their knowledge
of **/k/c** and **/d/d** to decode the words *catch* and *dog*.

**Think Aloud** *At the beginning of the word I see
the letter* d. *I know that* d *stands for* **/d/.** *In the
picture I see a dog. The word* dog *begins with* **/d/.** *This
word is* dog. *That makes sense in the sentence.*

**CONCEPTS
OF PRINT:
MATCH
SENTENCES**

Give small groups of children sentence strips. Invite them
to match each strip to the page in the book. Have them
point to each capital letter.

**ORAL
LANGUAGE:
ACTION
WORDS**

Together go through the book and read the words that tell
what each dog is doing. Invite children to act out these
words. Have children suggest and pantomime words for
other actions that the dogs might do.

**READ FOR
FLUENCY**

Invite children to read their High-Frequency Readers in a
small group. Have children discuss which dog trick they
like the best.

**READ AND
WRITE
INDEPENDENTLY**

**Journal** Place copies of the High-Frequency Readers in
the Reading Center. Children can read the book
independently or in small groups. Children can draw or
write in their Journals about the dog trick they liked best.

# CENTER WORKSHOPS

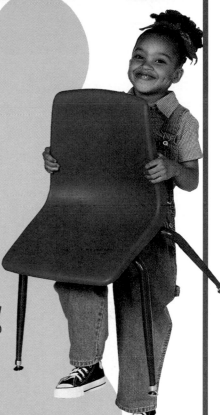

**Writing**

## Classroom Improvement

Talk together about how the classroom is organized. Work together to think of ways to reorganize the room to make it even better.

- When you've agreed on a way to reorganize the room or an area, write the group's ideas on a chart. Together, identify all of the tasks that need to be done. List each task on the chart.

- Help each group choose a task and work together on it. When done, encourage them to congratulate themselves on working together!

*Observation:* What problems do children identify in the room's organization? What suggestions do they make?

### MATERIALS

- Chart paper
- Markers

**Social Studies**

## Working Together Mural

Ask children to list places where people have fun working together. Make a list on chart paper. Possible suggestions might include *home, library, classroom, grocery store,* or *town*.

- Children can select one of the places and list all the ways that people might help one another there.

- Guide children to work together to make a mural of the place they selected, showing the different ways people work together.

*Observation:* What places do children suggest? What ways of working together do they identify?

### MATERIALS

- Paints
- Mural paper
- Chart paper
- Markers
- The 100th Day of School
- SourceCard

## DAY 8 OBJECTIVES

CHILDREN WILL:

- orally blend onsets and rimes
- review /h/h
- discuss animal sounds
- read and respond to *The Cow That Went OINK*
- write speech balloons
- chime in on repeated text
- engage in Center Workshops

## MATERIALS

- *The Cow That Went OINK*
- Chart or mural paper

# Share the Read Aloud

## DAILY PHONICS

## Consonant /h/h

### A PHONOLOGICAL AWARENESS

**Oral Blending** Say the following word parts aloud and ask children to blend them. Provide corrective feedback and modeling when necessary.

| | | |
|---|---|---|
| /h/. . . ot | /h/. . . orse | /h/. . . og |
| /h/. . . ome | /h/. . . at | /h/. . . and |

### B CONNECT SOUND-SPELLING

**Horses and Hamsters** Say the word *hog* as you write it on the chalkboard. Say it again, emphasizing the beginning sound **/h/.** Read aloud the following words: *hippo, lion, horse, hamster, tiger, hyena.* Invite children to *neigh* like a horse each time you say an animal's name that begins with **/h/.** Write the animals whose names begin with **/h/h** on the board. Have volunteers circle the letter *h* as you read the word together.

## Build Background

**ORAL LANGUAGE: FARM ANIMALS**

Ask children to share what they know about farm animals. What animals live on farms? Make a list on chart paper. Read the name of each animal. Ask children to repeat it and make the sound that animal makes.

**PREVIEW AND PREDICT**

Show the cover of the book and read the title and the author's and illustrator's names. Ask:

▶ **Is there anything funny about the title? What is it?**

▶ **What sound do most cows make?**

▶ **What do you think this story will be about?**

**SET A PURPOSE**

Show children the title page. Explain that this page also tells the name of the book and the author. Invite children to find the animals in the picture as they listen to the story.

## Share the Read Aloud

**MAKE STORY PREDICTIONS**

Share the pictures as you read the story aloud. Point out the speech balloons and explain that they show what the animals are saying.

Invite children to predict what will happen to the cow and pig as you read.

▶ **How do you think the other animals will act toward the pig?**

▶ **Now that the pig can oink, what do you think it will do?**

As you continue to read, acknowledge the predictions that children made.

**The Cow That Went OINK**

## Respond to the Literature

**TALK ABOUT IT**

**Share Personal Responses** Invite children to share their thoughts and feelings about the story.

▶ **What is your favorite part of the story?**

▶ **Why did the animals laugh at the cow and the pig?**

▶ **How did the cow and the pig help each other?**

▶ **How are the cow and the pig like Herman the helper?**

Children might enjoy responding to the book by singing a farm song such as *Old MacDonald*.

**THINK ABOUT IT**

**Theme Connection: Working Together** Talk about the problem that the cow and the pig had.

▶ **Why would oinking be a problem for a cow? Why would mooing be a problem for a pig?**

▶ **How would being able to moo *and* oink be good?**

▶ **How would the story be different if the cow and the pig did not help each other? How would the story be different if either one had given up?**

**MODIFY Instruction**

### ESL/ELD

▲ Ask English language learners how animals' voices are portrayed in children's first language. Does a cow say something other than "moo"? Does a pig say something other than "oink"? Invite children to record the animal sounds. **(USE AUDIO)**

## MODIFY
### Instruction

### GIFTED & TALENTED

✳ Challenge children to use speech balloons to write dialogue for the animals in the story. Have children work in groups to draw the characters and write something they think these characters would like to say to each other. **(WORK IN GROUPS)**

**ANIMAL SOUND SPEECH BALLOONS**

## Shared Writing

Talk about the speech balloons in the book. Invite children to make an animal sound mural.

- Brainstorm a list of animals. Read the list aloud and encourage children to make each animal's sound.
- Have children create a mural of the animals on their list. Help them to add speech balloons with the animals' sounds.
- Display the mural for everyone to enjoy. You may want to read it over together and have each child read the speech balloon he or she contributed.

## Repeated Reading

**CHIME IN ON ANIMAL SOUNDS**

Read the story again, letting children provide the animal sounds and laughter. Encourage children to comment on the story characters and how they are feeling throughout the story.

▶ **How do you think the cow feels when she hears the pig say** *moo***?**

▶ **What do you think about the way the other animals are acting towards the cow and pig?**

▶ **How do you think the cow and pig are feeling at the end of the story?**

**READ AND WRITE INDEPENDENTLY**

**Journal** Place *The Cow That Went OINK* in the Reading Center so children can enjoy it on their own. Suggest that children read or retell the story to a partner, using the book's illustrations to remind them of events. Children can write in their Journals about the cow and the pig.

##  Comprehension Check

**ACT IT OUT**

As you narrate the story, children can pretend to be the animals. Encourage them to behave like the animals in the story and to use the animals' movements and sounds.

# CENTER WORKSHOPS

### Cooking

## MATERIALS

- Animal-shaped cookie cutters
- 1 cup flour
- 1/4 cup butter
- 2 ounces cheese
- 1 beaten egg
- poppy seeds

## Animal Crackers

Have fun making animal crackers with children.

- Add the butter to the flour and mix until it has the texture of bread crumbs. Sift in shredded cheese. Add 2 tablespoons of the egg to make dough. Knead the dough lightly and roll it out.

- Invite children to cut animal shapes out of the dough. Place the crackers on baking sheets, and brush them with the remaining egg. Sprinkle the crackers with seeds. Bake 12–15 minutes and then let them cool. Let children make sounds for their animals before they eat them!

*Observation:* What animal shapes and sounds do children make?

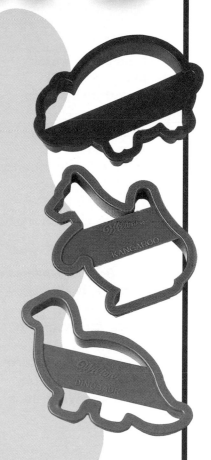

### Games

## MATERIALS

- Animal Sorting Cards
- Tape recorder

## Animal Sound March

Show the Animal Sorting Cards one at a time and encourage children to make each animal's sound. Tape-record the sounds children make.

- Place the animal pictures on a table or rug. Play the tape of the animal sounds that children made, pausing it after each sound. Encourage children to find the picture of the animal that makes the sound that they just heard.

*Observation:* What sounds do children make for each animal? How do they go about matching the animal sounds with pictures?

## DAY 9
## OBJECTIVES

**CHILDREN WILL:**

- orally segment words (beginning sounds)
- match letters in words
- review /h/h
- recognize sound-letter relationships
- review the high-frequency words
- read My Book: *We Clean Up*
- engage in Center Workshops

## MATERIALS

- *The Big Book of Rhymes and Rhythms,* p. 13
- ABC Card for *Hh*
- Sentence Strips for "To Market"
- *The Cow That Went OINK*
- My Book: *We Clean Up*
- My Read and Write Book, p. 11

**My Read and Write Book, p. 11**

For additional practice see *Scholastic Phonics K,* pp. 43–48. See also Sound and Letter book: *A Happy Hippo.*

# Sounds and Letters

DAILY PHONICS — and Read My Book

## Consonant /h/h

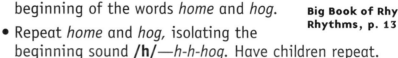

### Ⓐ PHONOLOGICAL AWARENESS

**Oral Segmentation: Beginning Sounds**
Open the *Big Book of Rhymes and Rhythms* and read "To Market" aloud.

**Big Book of Rhymes and Rhythms, p. 13**

- Ask children to raise their hands when they hear a word that begins with /h/ as in *hat.*

- Invite children to join in as you read the poem again. Encourage them to emphasize the /h/ sound at the beginning of the words *home* and *hog.*

- Repeat *home* and *hog,* isolating the beginning sound /h/—*h-h-hog.* Have children repeat.

### Ⓑ CONCEPTS OF PRINT

Put the Sentence Strips for "To Market" and a pocket chart in the Reading Center. Before you read the rhyme, let children group together the lines that begin with "To market . . ." and the lines that begin with "Home again. . . ."

| To market, to market, | Home again, home again, |
|---|---|
| To market, to market, | Home again, home again, |

Children can compare the lines to discover what is the same and what is different. Then read the rhyme together, one line at a time. Have volunteers find the Sentence Strip that shows that line and put it in the pocket chart.

## C CONNECT SOUND-SPELLING

**Alphabetic Principle** Remind children that the letter *Hh* stands for /h/ as in *hat.* Turn to the second page in *The Cow Went OINK.* Read the words *Moo-Ha* in the cow's speech balloon. Invite children to listen for the /h/ sound. Have volunteers point to the letter that makes the /h/ sound in *Ha.*

Then invite children to read the words *Moo-Ha* in all of the speech balloons on the third page. Track the print as you read, stopping briefly at the letter *H.* Encourage children to emphasize the /h/ sound.

**ABC Book** Explain to children that they are going to make a new page for their own ABC book. Have children make suggestions of animals, objects, and people whose names begin with /h/. When the list is complete, invite children to work together to create *Hh* pages.

**Label Hand Prints** Invite children to make a hand prints poster using finger paint. Help them label the prints with each child's name and the word *hands.* Invite children to read the poster to identify each other's hands.

## D VOCABULARY: HIGH-FREQUENCY WORDS

Write the following sentences on the chalkboard. Tell children that only some of the sentences contain the high-frequency word *my.* If necessary, review the word *my* using the read-spell-write method.

Read each sentence aloud. Ask children to listen for and find the high-frequency word *my.* Invite volunteers to raise their hands when they hear *my* and to draw a square around the word.

> I see clouds.
>
> Do you like my smile?
>
> I ride a bike.
>
> Are you my friend?

---

### ESL/ELD

▲ On the chalkboard write examples of words that begin with the letter *h.* As you write them, pronounce each word and have children repeat the word. Note that in Spanish and French the *h* is silent. **(ASSIST IN PROCESS)**

### TECHNOLOGY

Ask children to write each word horizontally on the **WiggleWorks Plus** Magnet Board as pictured. Let them write *H* over each vowel and add another letter beneath the vowel to complete a word vertically. Offer clues such as: *something to wear on your head; not him but _____; I _____ in the closet; not hers but _____.*

The rhyme in the *Big Book of Rhymes and Rhythms* is available on the **Sounds of Phonics** audiocassette.

**We Clean Up**

# Read My Book

**INTRODUCE THE BOOK**

Let children know that they are going to get their own book that they can read on their own and take home.

▶ **How do you help clean up in school?**

▶ **How do you help clean up at home?**

**PREVIEW AND PREDICT**

Pass out copies of *We Clean Up*. Read the author's and illustrator's names. Ask children about the cover.

▶ **What might this book be about?**

**READ TOGETHER**

Read *We Clean Up* with children, tracking the print as you go. Guide children to read along in their copies and to think about how the boy in the story might feel as he cleans up with his father.

**PHONICS**

To review the letter *Dd,* ask children to say the words *Dad* and *done* aloud.

▶ **What sound do you hear at the beginning of the words? What letter stands for that sound?**

Help children find these words in their books.

**READ AND WRITE INDEPENDENTLY**

**Journal** Encourage children to read *We Clean Up* on their own. Provide crayons for children to color the illustrations. Have children write about how they help clean up at home.

**HOME/SCHOOL CONNECTION**

Children can take home their My Book to share with family members and friends. Suggest that children make a book with family members about the ways they all help to keep their home clean.

# CENTER WORKSHOPS

## Alphabet

### A Heap of *Hh*'s!

Children can trace their hands and then sort their hand prints.

Invite children to make *Hh* with all kinds of materials. They can trace them in sand, form them with clay, and draw them with finger paints.

*Observation:* Notice how easily children are forming the letter *Hh*.

**MATERIALS**

- *Hh* Alphabet Cards
- Sand
- Clay
- Finger paints
- Oaktag paper
- Markers
- Drawing paper

## Health & Fitness

### *Hh* Charades!

Guide children to organize themselves into teams to play *Hh* word charades. Each team can think of an *Hh* word to act out. They might choose to imitate a verb such as *hop* or *hum*, the name of an animal such as *hamster*, *hippo*, or *horse*, or other *Hh* words, such as *happy* or *hungry*. Invite other teams to guess the word.

As a variation, a team might think of an *Hh* word and challenge another team to act it out.

*Observation:* How do children work together to act out their team's *Hh* words? Which children like to perform large-motor movements?

**MATERIALS**

- None

## DAY 10 OBJECTIVES

**CHILDREN WILL:**

- compare and contrast books they've read
- write a group language experience chart
- listen for alliteration
- review /h/h and /g/g
- create a project: Daily Menu

## MATERIALS

- *The 100th Day of School*
- *Herman the Helper*
- *Tortillas*
- *The Cow That Went OINK*

## TECHNOLOGY

 Children may tape record their responses to the three stories they have heard. Children might interview one another about how they have fun helping.

# Put It All Together

## Sum It Up

**HOW WE HELP**

Remind children that they have been reading and talking about different ways people can have fun helping each other. Encourage children to continue thinking and talking about people who have fun helping each other—friends, family members, people in school, and people in the community.

**ORAL LANGUAGE: SING A SONG**

Sing "The More We Help Each Other" to the tune of "The More We Get Together." Invite children to stand together in a circle and sing along.

### The More We Help Each Other

The more we help each other,

each other, each other,

the more we help each other,

the happier we'll be!

For your friends are my friends,

and my friends are your friends.

The more we help each other,

the happier we'll be!

Encourage children to talk about times they've had fun helping.

▶ **Who do you like to help? How do you like to help? How do you feel when you help?**

**COMPARE AND CONTRAST CHART**

# Language Experience Chart

Display the books children have read during the previous nine days. Invite them to ask any questions they have.

Make a language chart called "It's Fun To Help!" Talk together about how people have fun helping each other in the books they've read. Write children's responses on the language chart. The chart may look something like the one shown below.

Children can illustrate the chart, making it a decorative mural. Display the chart as part of the documentation for what children have been doing.

**MODIFY Instruction**

## EXTRA HELP

■ In order for children to compare the stories, guide them to identify the goal in each case. For example, you may ask, "Why do the cow and the pig help each other learn how to make the correct sound?" Encourage children to imagine and discuss what would have happened in each case if just one character had done all the work. **(COMPARE AND CONTRAST)**

## It's Fun To Help!

**The 100th Day of School**

Lots of children have fun celebrating the 100th day of school together. They work together to decorate, make cookies, play games, and do other activities.

**Herman the Helper**

An octopus named Herman helps his friends and family members out of trouble so they can have fun in the ocean.

**The Cow That Went OINK**

A cow and a pig help each other learn a new language.

*Observation*

How are the children doing? Are they:

• working together to make a language chart?

• recognizing how the stories relate to the theme?

• recalling many details of the stories?

# Maintenance

## MODIFY Instruction

### ESL/ELD

▲ When children are having difficulty hearing a beginning sound, say the word slowly. Point out the position of your lips and tongue when making the sound. You may also ask children if they feel a burst of air or a vibration in their throat when making the sound themselves. **(MODEL)**

**Ⓐ PHONOLOGICAL AWARENESS**

**Alliteration** Say aloud the following alliterative phrases about animals. Invite children to notice how each phrase is the same. Encourage them to mention that each phrase tells something about an animal and that both words begin with the same sound. Read the phrases again. Have children emphasize and identify the beginning sounds.

- Happy Hippo
- Heavy Hamster
- Hungry Horse
- Gorgeous Gorilla
- Goofy Gopher
- Golden Goose

**Ⓑ PHONICS ACTIVITY**

**Alliteration Zoo** Write the alliterative phrases above on the chalkboard. Together read them aloud. Invite children to pick one phrase that begins with *Gg* and another that begins with *Hh*. Have them illustrate the animal described in each phrase. You may want to have a group discussion about how each animal described might look. Help children write the phrases on their drawings. Ask them to circle the beginning letters *Gg* and *Hh*.

# WEEKS 1 AND 2
# PROJECT

## Daily Menu

**A**s children have shared the books in the past two weeks they've seen people having fun working and eating together. Point out that eating and making food is one way people work and enjoy being together. Children can create a daily menu chart that can be used throughout the year.

Talk together about the different foods people ate in *The 100th Day of School* and *Tortillas*. Then talk about how restaurants list the foods they serve.

Write "Daily Menu" on the top of a piece of oaktag. Make rows for each of the meals children have in your class.

Ask children to name the first meal that the class has each day and write it on the chart. Children can work together to draw a picture that represents that meal. Ask children what they ate for that meal, and write each response on a separate strip of oaktag. Encourage children to decorate the strip with pictures of the foods named.

Do the same for each meal you have, adding new food labels each day.

***Observation:*** Which meals and foods do children name?

### MATERIALS

- **Oaktag with Velcro™ strips**
- **Crayons**
- **Markers**
- **Scissors**
- **Strips of oaktag**

### BENCHMARKS

**Monitor children's progress. Are they**

- working together and helping one another?
- participating in composing group lists?
- recognizing concepts of print in the stories?

# WEEKS
# 3 AND 4

# Kindergarten Goals
## for Weeks 3 and 4

## Oral Language/ Vocabulary
- participating in group discussions
- building vocabulary for fruits, vegetables, color, shape
- exploring story vocabulary

## Reading
- building alphabetic knowledge
- participating actively in shared reading
- engaging in emergent reading
- exploring concepts of print
- investigating cause/effect
- exploring characters' feelings
- sequencing story events
- making predictions
- investigating picture details
- understanding speech balloons
- recognizing story plot
- reading high-frequency words

## Writing
- writing about favorite foods
- creating compound words
- writing letters: *Ii, Jj*
- writing welcoming phrases
- recording story sequence
- writing directions
- creating animal rhymes
- engaging in shared writing
- writing independently in Journals

## Listening/Speaking/ Viewing
- listening to read alouds
- listening to rhyme and rhythm
- developing phonological awareness
- listening for story pattern
- listening for information
- listening to follow directions
- discussing problem/solution
- dramatizing a story
- singing songs
- engaging in conversations
- sharing personal experiences
- demonstrating visual literacy

## Daily Phonics: *Ii* and *Jj*
- reciting classic poems, songs, and nursery rhymes
- naming and recognizing the letters
- recognizing sound/letter relationships
- generating words with /i/, /j/
- decoding words using /i/*i*, /j/*j*

## Center Workshops and Project
- acquiring world knowledge through cross-curricular activities
- making a big book of recipes

# RESOURCES

## Big Book

### Meet the Author/Illustrator

Bruce Degen has illustrated many more books than he has written. "I'm a very slow writer and a very fast illustrator," he says. *Jamberry* was inspired by joyous childhood memories.

Available as audiocassette

## Big Book of Rhymes and Rhythms

For teaching phonological awareness, the alphabet, and concepts of print.

- "If All the World"
- "Jack Be Nimble"

Available as audiocassette

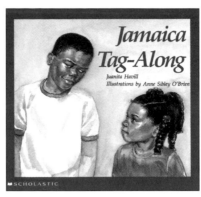

## Read Aloud

### Meet the Author

Juanita Havill has been making up stories since earliest childhood. Even before she could write, she dictated stories to her mother!

### Meet the Illustrator

Anne Sibley O'Brien has collaborated with Juanita Havill on several Jamaica books.

## Read Aloud

### Meet the Author/Illustrator

Jan Ormerod was inspired by family life to create books. Her husband worked as a librarian at the time their first child, Sophie, was born. Sophie's interest in the books her father brought home encouraged Ormerod to begin creating books.

## ABC Book

### Meet the Author/Illustrator

Lois Ehlert loves collage because it lets her change her mind about where things go. She cuts and arranges fabric and paper pieces, then glues them down.

**Side One**

**Side Two**

## SourceCard

- What are these people doing?
- Jam Sandwich

## High-Frequency Reader

## Storytelling

**"The Great Big Enormous Turnip"**

a Russian tale

**My Read and Write Book**

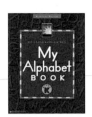

**My Alphabet Book**

**ESL/ELD Teaching Guide**

## My Books

To take home to share.

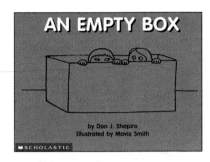

# Introducing the Mentor

Kwaku Twumasi is proud of his pizzas. He flattens the dough and then adds the toppings. Many of his pizzas are ordered for takeout dinners. Siam, the delivery boy, delivers Kwaku's pizzas to hungry customers.

# DAYS AT A GLANCE

## WEEKS 3 AND 4

| | Daily Phonics | Literature | Shared Writing | Workshops and Projects |
|---|---|---|---|---|
| **DAY 1** | Phonological Awareness: Oral Segmentation<br><br>Review /f/*f*, /g/*g*, /h/*h* | *Eating the Alphabet* by Lois Ehlert | Describe Fruits and Vegetables | Cooking: Apple Time!<br><br>Art: Paint a Still Life! |
| **DAY 2** | **Vowel /i/*i***<br>Phonological Awareness: Oral Segmentation | *Jamberry* by Bruce Degen | Create Compound Words | Social Studies: Create Berryland!<br><br>Music & Movement: Making Music! |
| **DAY 3** | **Vowel /i/*i***<br>Phonological Awareness: Alliteration<br><br>Introduce Sound-Spelling | *Jamberry* by Bruce Degen<br><br>**High-Frequency Reader:** *The Band* | Concepts of Print: Environmental Print<br><br>Write *Ii*<br><br>Make a Class Book | Art: Make Clayberry Magnets!<br><br>Cooking: "Berry" Good Fruit Ice |
| **DAY 4** | **Vowel /i/*i***<br>Phonological Awareness: Oral Blending<br><br>Review Sound-Spelling | *Jamaica Tag-Along* by Juanita Havill illustrated by Anne Sibley O'Brien  | Write Welcoming Messages | Blocks: Castle Creations<br><br>Music & Movement: Being Partners |
| **DAY 5** | **Vowel /i/*i***<br>Phonological Awareness: Rhyme<br><br>Maintain Sound-Spelling | *"If All the World"* a rhyme <br><br>*Eating the Alphabet*<br><br>**My Book:** *An Empty Box* | Concepts of Print: Word Boundaries<br><br>High-Frequency Word: *the* | Dramatic Play: Act Out *Ii*'s!<br><br>Alphabet: Form Those *Ii*'s! |

| | Daily Phonics | Literature | Shared Writing | Workshops and Projects |
|---|---|---|---|---|
| **DAY 6** | **Consonant /j/ j** Phonological Awareness: Auditory Discrimination | **"The Great Big Enormous Turnip"** a Russian tale by Alexei Tolstoi | Record Story Sequence | Art: Story Map<br><br>Math: How Much Could It Weigh? |
| **DAY 7** | **Consonant /j/ j** Phonological Awareness: Alliteration<br><br>Introduce Sound-Spelling | **SourceCard** What Are These People Doing? Jam Sandwich<br><br>**High-Frequency Reader:** *The Band* | Write Directions<br><br>Write *Jj* | Cooking: Making Jam Sandwiches<br><br>Social Studies: Photograph Fun |
| **DAY 8** | **Consonant /j/ j** Phonological Awareness: Oral Blending<br><br>Review Sound-Spelling | *The Story of Chicken Licken* by Jan Ormerod    READ ALOUD | Create Rhyming Animal Names | Art: Make Animal Faces!<br><br>Health & Fitness: Fowl Play |
| **DAY 9** | **Consonant /j/ j** Phonological Awareness: Oral Segmentation<br><br>Maintain Sound-Spelling | **"Jack Be Nimble"** a nursery rhyme<br><br>**My Book:** *Our Snowman* | Concepts of Print: Recognize Words<br><br>High-Frequency Words | Games: Play with *Jj!*<br><br>Math: Judging Juice! |
| **DAY 10** | Phonological Awareness: Rhyme<br><br>Phonics Maintenance | **Review Books from Weeks 3 and 4** | Make a Compare and Contrast Chart | Project: "Big Book of Recipes" |

## DAY 1 OBJECTIVES

**CHILDREN WILL:**

- orally segment words (beginning sounds)
- review consonants /f/f, /g/g, and /h/h
- talk about fruits and vegetables
- focus on *Ii, Jj*
- read and respond to *Eating the Alphabet*
- write describing words
- create a TV commercial
- engage in Center Workshops

## MATERIALS

- *Eating the Alphabet*

## GUIDED READING

To conclude each day's reading session, meet with guided reading groups. You might use Scholastic's Guided Reading Library or other books in your library.

# Share the ABC Book

## DAILY PHONICS

## Warm-Up: Wordplay

### Ⓐ PHONOLOGICAL AWARENESS

**Going to Grandma's** Invite children to play a quick game of I'm going to Grandma's. Have them complete the sentence **I'm going to Grandma's and I'm bringing** _____ with the name of something that begins with **/f/, /g/,** or **/h/.**

### Ⓑ PHONICS MAINTENANCE

**Consonants /f/f, /g/g, /h/h** Have children chant the alphabet in order as you page through *Eating the Alphabet*. Stop briefly on the pages containing the letters *Ff, Gg,* and *Hh.* Ask children to say the sound—**/f/, /g/,** or **/h/**—that each letter stands for and name the vegetables pictured.

## Build Background

**ORAL LANGUAGE: UNUSUAL FRUITS AND VEGETABLES**

Bring in some fruits and vegetables or pictures of fruits and vegetables that may be unfamiliar to children. Show the items one at a time, asking children to suggest possible names and then telling them the real ones. Some unusual fruits or vegetables that appear in the ABC book include radicchio, quince, jicama, kohlrabi, star fruit, ugli fruit, endive, gooseberry, and pomegranate.

Cut open some of the fruits and vegetables so children can see what's inside. Then enjoy them later as a snack.

**PREVIEW AND PREDICT**

Show children the cover of the ABC book, reading the title and the name of the author/illustrator.

▶ **Which fruits and vegetables do you see? Which do you see the inside of? Which fruits have red parts? green parts?**

**SET A PURPOSE**

Invite children to look for some of the unusual fruits and vegetables discussed in the book.

# Read the ABC Book

**ALPHABETIC KNOWLEDGE:**
*Ii* AND *Jj*

Read together *Eating the Alphabet*. Name the letter or letters on each page, and make up clues for each food, encouraging children to name the fruits and vegetables. For example, "What is the small yellowish fruit?" *(apricot)* and "What is the green vegetable with the pointy leaves?" *(artichoke)*

When you come to *Ii* and *Jj* page, help children identify the upper- and lowercase letters. Then have them name the vegetable that begins with *Ii*—*indian corn*. Name the vegetables for *Jj*—*jicama* and *jalapeno*. Tell children that *Jj* at the beginning of these vegetables has a different sound. Explain that the common sound for *Jj* is /j/ as in *juice*.

**Eating the Alphabet**

# Respond to the Literature

**TALK ABOUT IT**

**Share Personal Responses** Talk with children about the ABC book, letting them ask questions and share comments. Remind children to raise their hand during the discussion.

▶ **Which pictures did you like best? Why?**

▶ **Would you like to taste any new fruits or vegetables? Which ones?**

Model some questions children might ask about the fruits and vegetables, such as where they grow. Show them how to use the glossary to answer their questions.

**THINK ABOUT IT**

**Focus on Letters** Encourage children to talk about fruits and vegetables that they particularly enjoy and special ways to serve them. You might list children's suggestions on a chart.

▶ **Is your favorite fruit or vegetable mentioned in the book?**

▶ **If it is, which letter does it begin with? If it is not in the book, on which letter page would it appear if we added it to the book?**

## ESL/ELD

▲ Provide children acquiring English with additional opportunities to practice the names of fruits and vegetables. Pair up the children, and assign a different color to each pair. Read the book again, asking children to pay particular attention to the fruits and vegetables that are the color that their group was assigned. Then name a color and ask children in that group to list fruits and vegetables of that color. **(PICTURE CLUES)**

## Shared Writing

**DESCRIBE FRUITS AND VEGETABLES**

Encourage children to name fruits or vegetables that they like to eat. Write children's names and the fruit or vegetables they like on a chart. Ask them to suggest words to describe each fruit or vegetable and add the words to the chart. For example: furry (peach), green (grape), or skinny (carrot).

• Children can illustrate the chart with pictures of themselves and the fruit or vegetable they named.

• They then can write about their favorite fruits or vegetables and develop stories about them.

## Repeated Reading

**FOCUS ON LETTERS AND THEIR SOUNDS**

Reread the ABC book with children. Encourage them to name the letters on each page and to identify the fruits and vegetables. Help children notice the differences in the upper- and lowercase forms of each letter.

**READ AND WRITE INDEPENDENTLY**

**Journal** Encourage children to read *Eating the Alphabet* on their own or in small groups. Invite children to draw and write in their Journals about a fruit and vegetable store.

## ✓ Comprehension Check

**ACT IT OUT**

Invite children to create and act out a TV commercial for a favorite fruit or vegetable. Remind them of advertisements they may have seen for milk and for breakfast cereals. Encourage them to focus on what would make someone want to buy the fruit or vegetable.

If possible, videotape children's commercials. They will enjoy seeing themselves perform!

# CENTER WORKSHOPS

## Apple Time!

Write the recipe for dried apples on chart paper, and post it in the Cooking Center.

- Follow the recipe with children, encouraging them to work together. Over the four days that the apple slices are drying, encourage children to notice how the slices change. Record their comments on a chart. When the slices are done, they will be chewy. Serve the apples for a snack.

- Alternatively, you might dry the apples in the cafeteria oven at 150 degrees. Cool and serve.

*Observation:* What changes do children notice in the apples as they dry?

### MATERIALS

- Charted recipe
- Apples
- Plastic knives
- Cooling rack
- Cheesecloth

> **— DRIED APPLES —**
> 1. Wash and core apples.
> 2. Cut the apples into slices with plastic knives.
> 3. Place the apples on a cooling rack so that air can circulate around them.
> 4. Cover the rack with cheesecloth. Then move it to a sunny place.
> 5. Let the apple slices dry for 4 days.

## Paint a Still Life!

Show children still life paintings of fruits and vegetables, done in a variety of artistic styles.

- Put the bowl of fruits and vegetables where children can see it. Show them the art materials you've assembled and let them choose some to create what they see.

- Create a little art gallery where children can view the finished works.

- Talk about why the pictures look different even though everyone was looking at the same thing.

*Observation:* Notice which art materials children choose to create what they see.

### MATERIALS

- Reproductions of art still lifes
- A bowl of fruits and vegetables
- Construction paper
- Scissors
- Paste or glue
- Markers
- Paints

## DAY 2 OBJECTIVES

**CHILDREN WILL:**

- develop phonological awareness
- recognize /i/
- listen to and participate in a reading of *Jamberry*
- speak about funny made-up words
- create compound words
- engage in Center Workshops

## MATERIALS

- *Jamberry*
- **My Read and Write Book,** p. 12

## TECHNOLOGY

 The Big Book is available on audiocassette in the Literacy Place Listening Center.

 The song is available on the **Sounds of Phonics** audiocassette.

# Share the Big Book

 DAILY PHONICS

## Vowel /i/i

### PHONOLOGICAL AWARENESS

**Song** Read aloud the title of the song "If I Could Play." Say the word *if,* isolating the beginning sound: *i-i-if.* Have children repeat.

Then sing or play the song, using hand motions to demonstrate playing the instruments. Invite children to sing along. During later singings have children exaggerate the initial **/i/** in *if.*

### If I Could Play

If I could play the piano,
This is the way I would play.
If I had a guitar,
I would strum the strings this way.
If I had a trumpet,
I'd toot to make a tune.
But, if I played a drum,
I'd go BOOM, BOOM, BOOM.

## Build Background

**ORAL LANGUAGE: BERRIES**

Encourage children to discuss different kinds of berries.

▶ **What color berries have you seen?**

▶ **What do the berries feel like in your mouth?**

▶ **Which jams made from berries do you like?**

**PREVIEW AND PREDICT**

Show children the cover of *Jamberry*. Read the title and the name of the author/illustrator, tracking the print.

▶ **What do you think the title of the book means?**

# Read the Big Book

**LISTEN TO
THE RHYME
AND RHYTHM**

Encourage children to talk about what's happening in the illustrations on the half-title page, the title page, and the dedication page.

Read the book. Emphasize the pattern of rhythm and rhyme by reading it in a lilting voice and having fun with it!

# Respond to the Literature

**TALK
ABOUT IT**

**Share Personal Responses** Talk with children about their favorite part of the book. Share your favorite part, too.

Recall with children that the author made up lots of funny, new words from the word *berry*, such as *canoeberry*, *pawberry*, and *quackberry*.

► **Which were your favorite words? Why?**

► **Which picture was the most fun to look at? Why?**

► **How did the boy feel about the journey that he and the bear took? How would you feel if you were the boy?**

**THINK
ABOUT IT**

**Made-up Words** Talk with children about the different *berry*-words used in the book. Some are names for real kinds of berries, while others are simply fun, made-up words. Help children discover which are which by making a chart.

You might also explain the double meanings of the word *jam* as used in the book: "a sweet food to spread on bread," and "to play music, usually jazz, making it up as you go along." You may also want to explain that *razzamatazz* means "excitement" or "a big flashy display."

| real words | made-up words |
|------------|---------------|
| blueberry | shoeberry |
| strawberry | hatberry |
| blackberry | canoeberry |
| raspberry | pawberry |

Jamberry

## MODIFY Instruction

### ESL/ELD

▲ Bring in pictures or samples of different kinds of berries. Also, bring in jars of jam, preferably made of berries. Ask: *Do you eat berries? What kind? Did you ever pick berries? Where? Can you find the real and made-up berry words in the story?* Ask children to pronounce each of the words they learn. **(GUIDED QUESTIONS)**

**My Read and Write Book, p. 12**

## Shared Writing

**CREATE COMPOUND WORDS**

Show children the cover of the Big Book. Point out that the title *Jamberry* is made up of two smaller words: *jam* and *berry*. Invite children to create compound words like those in the book, using made-up berry words.

- To get children started, write a few made-up berry words from the book, such as *jazzberry, shoeberry,* and *berryband*, on chart paper.
- Add the words children make up to the chart.
- Invite them to create illustrations for their made-up words.

## Repeated Reading

**FOCUS ON RHYMES**

As you reread the book, pause before reading the word that will complete a rhyme and encourage children to supply it. If children don't offer it quickly, have them find clues in the picture to help them guess or remember the word.

**READ AND WRITE INDEPENDENTLY**

**Journal** Place copies of *Jamberry* in your Reading Center along with the audiocassette. Encourage children to read *Jamberry* on their own or in small groups. Encourage children to have conversations with one another about their favorite parts of the book.

## ☑ Comprehension Check

**ACT IT OUT**

Invite volunteers to act out one or more of the scenes in *Jamberry*. One child might play the bear and another the boy, or different children might play these parts on different pages. Other children might act out the smaller parts of the lambs, ponies, geese, rabbits, and elephants. Remind children to speak their parts clearly and loudly.

# CENTER WORKSHOPS

## Social Studies

### MATERIALS

- **Crayons or markers**
- **Large paper**

### Create Berryland!

Invite children to draw festive scenes like those in the book, featuring different kinds of items decorated with berries. Children might think of various names for their scenes, such as Cityberry, Forestberry, Highwayberry, Schoolberry, and Circusberry.

Remind children that the author/illustrator of *Jamberry* used berries to decorate such things as clothing, signs, flags, and buildings. There are berries in things and on things. Each child can add his or her own unique berry place to the paper.

When children are finished, talk about how each child contributed something to Berryland.

*Observation:* What items do children illustrate with berries?

## Music & Movement

### MATERIALS

- **Recycled coffee cans**
- **Cardboard tubes**
- **Wax paper**
- **Construction paper**
- **Markers**
- **Paper punch**
- **Rubber bands**
- **Stapler**

### Making Music!

The characters in *Jamberry* have great fun with music. Children can choose an instrument to make.

- **Kazoo** Children can punch a hole near one end of a paper-towel tube, and cover it with waxed paper. Children can hum into the open end.

- **Maraca** Children can pinch one end of a cardboard tube and staple it closed. They can put pebbles inside, staple the other end, and shake!

- **Drum** Cut construction paper to fit around a coffee can. Children can draw designs on their paper and glue it around the can. Attach the coffee can lid and let children beat the drum.

*Observation:* How do children work together to create and play their musical instruments?

# DAY 3

## DAY 3 OBJECTIVES

**CHILDREN WILL:**

- listen for alliteration
- recognize vowel /i/i
- write the letter *Ii*
- reread *Jamberry*
- explore environmental print
- identify high-frequency word: *the*
- read the High-Frequency Reader: *The Band*
- engage in Center Workshops

## MATERIALS

- *Jamberry*
- High-Frequency Reader: *The Band*
- My Alphabet Book, p. 11
- My Read and Write Book, pp. 13–15

The Big Book is available on audiocassette in the Literacy Place Listening Center.

My Alphabet Book, p. 11

# Revisit the Big Book

## Vowel /i/i

### Ⓐ PHONOLOGICAL AWARENESS

**Alliteration** Ask children to recite this alliterative sentence after you.

***Isabel is in the igloo.***

Repeat the alliterative sentence together, and have children count the number of times they hear **/i/**.

### Ⓑ CONNECT SOUND-SPELLING

**Introduce Vowel /i/i** Page through *Eating the Alphabet* until you get to the *Ii* page. Point out to children that the letter *Ii* stands for **/i/** as in **Indian corn**. Ask children to say the sound with you.

- On the chalkboard, write the sentence *Isabel is in the igloo*. Read it and circle each initial *Ii*.

## Letter Formation

**WRITE THE LETTER**

Write *Ii* on the chalkboard. Point out the capital and small forms of the letter. Model how to write the letter using the rhymes provided below.

- Have children write both forms of the letter. Ask children to make the letter's sound as they practice writing.
- Observe how children hold their pencils and position their papers.

**I**

**One long line down,**
**Straight till you stop.**
*(Pull straight down.)*
**Then a short line at the bottom,**
**And one at the top.**
*(Pull across top and bottom, left to right.)*

**i**

**Make a straight line down,**
**Shorter than before,**
*(Start in the middle of the space and pull straight down to the line.)*
**Then make a little dot**
**Over the top.**
*(Add a dot.)*

## Reread the Big Book

**OPTIONS**

**Focus on Illustrations** Share *Jamberry* with children again, encouraging them to look carefully at the pictures as you read. Ask children what unusual details they see.

▶ **What strange things do you see growing on the tree?** *(page 7, bread)*

▶ **What's floating on the water like a lily pad?** *(page 7, pies)*

▶ **What are the posts on the bridge made of?** *(page 8, jam jars)*

**Author's Purpose** Read the dedication page of the Big Book again.

▶ **Who might be the "special Berry Picker and the two Little Berries?"**

Explain that the author, Bruce Degen, dedicated *Jamberry* to his wife and two sons. Let children know that as a small boy, Bruce Degen picked pails full of berries in the fields with his grandparents.

**READ AND WRITE INDEPENDENTLY**

**Journal** Place copies of *Jamberry* in the Reading Center for children to read alone or in small groups. Children can write in their Journals about times they have picked, bought, or eaten berries.

Jamberry

## Concepts of Print

**ENVIRONMENTAL PRINT**

Talk with children about the many examples of environmental print included in the illustrations of *Jamberry*.

• On page 8, the rowboat named *Jellybean II.*

• On page 19, the train car is labeled "Boys-in-Berries R.R." (Help them understand the word play: boysenberries/Boys-in-Berries.)

• On page 21, there's a railroad crossing sign; on page 23, the train station is named *Berryland;* on pages 24–25, there are two signs.

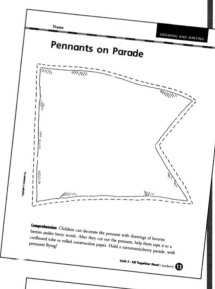

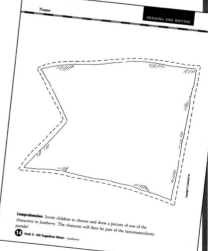

**My Read and Write Book, pp. 13–14.**

**The Band**

## Read High-Frequency Reader

**INTRODUCE THE BOOK**

Show the book *The Band.* Read the title and the author's name. Read aloud the sign that says "Parade at 7:00 PM."

▶ **Have you ever seen a parade? What do you think the children in the picture are doing? What do you think this book will be about?**

**HIGH-FREQUENCY WORD: *the***

- Write the sentence stem *Can you see the _____?* on the board. Underline the word *the.* Then write the word *the* on a note card. Read it aloud.
- Display the card and have children read the word.
- Help children spell it aloud, clapping on each letter.
- Ask children to write it in the air as they state aloud each letter.

Review the high-frequency words *can, you,* and *see.* Ask volunteers to find them on the Word Wall and read them aloud. Then invite children to complete the question by asking about something that they see. Write each new question on the board.

Add the card for *the* to the Word Wall.

**SHARE THE HIGH-FREQUENCY READER**

Read the story aloud, tracking the print. After each two-page spread, have children point to the instrument and tell where the child is practicing.

- The story also reviews consonants **/g/** and **/h/.** Help children use their knowledge of these sound-spellings to decode the words *guitar, harmonica,* and *horn.*

**SHARED WRITING**

Invite children to make a class book called *The Things We Can See.*

- Ask each child to draw a picture of something they see in the classroom or out the classroom window. Help children write and complete the sentence *I can see the _____* under their picture. Bind the pages into a book and share it with the class.

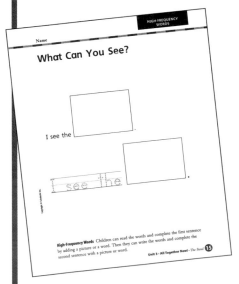

**My Read and Write Book, p. 15**

# CENTER WORKSHOPS

**Art**

## Make Clayberry Magnets!

(Note: To make craft clay, combine 1 cup corn starch, 2 cups baking soda, and $1\frac{1}{4}$ cups water. Cook until thickened to a dough-like consistency. Knead on a pastry board and store in a plastic bag.)

**Individuals** Children can make berry refrigerator magnets. If possible, have real berries for children to use as models.

1. Children roll out the clay, then cut out a berry shape.

2. When the shapes are dry, children can paint their berries. Let the paint dry.

3. Supervise as children glue magnets to the back of their painted berries.

*Observation:* How do children make their clayberries?

### MATERIALS

- Craft clay
- Rolling pins
- Plastic knives
- Paints
- Small magnets
- Glue

**Cooking**

## "Berry" Good Fruit Ice

Supervise as children make berry ice.

1. Help children puree the berries.

2. If you wish, pour the puree through a sieve to get rid of the seeds.

3. Help children put the puree back into the blender, and add the sugar, lemon juice, and water. Blend for 2 seconds.

4. Freeze the puree in the ice cube tray.

5. To serve, children can whirl the frozen cubes in the blender until they have a velvety slush. Serve right away!

*Observation:* Which children choose to work together in the Cooking Center?

### MATERIALS

Serves 6 children:
- 4 cups berries
- 1/4 cup sugar
- 1 tablespoon lemon juice
- 1/2 cup water
- Blender
- Sieve
- Ice-cube tray

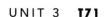

## DAY 4 OBJECTIVES

**CHILDREN WILL:**

- orally blend word parts
- review vowel /i/i
- read and respond to *Jamaica Tag-Along*
- recognize characters' feelings
- recognize cause and effect
- write words that welcome
- engage in Center Workshops

## MATERIALS

- *Jamaica Tag-Along*
- **My Read and Write Book,** pp. 16–17

## TECHNOLOGY

Have children reillustrate their favorite part of the story using the drawing tools in the **WiggleWorks Plus** Write area. Children may want to print their work to share with their family.

# Share the Read Aloud

## Vowel /i/i

### Ⓐ PHONOLOGICAL AWARENESS

**Oral Blending** Read aloud the following word parts, and ask children to put the sounds together to say the word. Provide corrective feedback and modeling when necessary.

| | | |
|---|---|---|
| /d/ . . . id | /l/ . . . id | /b/. . . ig |
| /f/ . . . ig | /h/. . . im | /f/. . . it |

### Ⓑ CONNECT SOUND-SPELLING

**Add a Sound** Write *in, it,* and *is* on the chalkboard and ask volunteers to circle the letter *i* in each word. Remind children that the letter *i* stands for /i/.

Add an initial consonant to each *i* word to make the words *fin, fit, hit,* and *his.* Pronounce the first sound separately, then blend the word, /f/. . . *it.* Do the same for each word, asking children to repeat the process as you track each word. Point out that *i* has the same sound even though it is now in the middle of the word.

## Build Background

**ORAL LANGUAGE: TAGGING ALONG**

Encourage children to talk about what happens when conflicts arise during their play time.

▶ **How do you solve problems during play?**

Talk about what it means to tag along.

**PREVIEW AND PREDICT**

Show children the cover of the book. Read the title and the author's and illustrator's names, pointing to each as you read. Encourage children to share their ideas about what the story might be about.

▶ **Have you ever heard a story about Jamaica?**

▶ **What does the expression on the boy's face tell you?**

## Share the Read Aloud

**FOCUS ON CHARACTER**

Read *Jamaica Tag-Along* with expression, paying special attention to the characters' moods and tones of voice in the dialogue sections of the story. Encourage children to think about how each of the characters, especially Jamaica, might be feeling throughout the story.

## Respond to the Literature

**TALK ABOUT IT**

**Share Personal Responses** Invite children to think aloud about the characters' feelings.

▶ How do you think Jamaica felt when Ossie told her to stay out of the way?

**Jamaica Tag-Along**

▶ How do you think Jamaica felt when she told Berto to stay away from her castle?

▶ Have you ever felt like Jamaica?

**THINK ABOUT IT**

**Understand Story Events** Generate a discussion about story content.

▶ What caused Jamaica to feel sad?

▶ Why didn't Jamaica want Berto to help her build the sand castle at first? What made her change her mind?

▶ How did the author show that Jamaica was aware of her feelings?

▶ Why did Jamaica let Ossie help with the sand castle? What do you think Ossie will say the next time Jamaica wants to play with him?

**MODIFY**
**Instruction**

**EXTRA HELP**

■ As children respond to the story, suggest that they express their ideas nonverbally. For example, you may want to invite a child to show how Jamaica felt when Ossie told her to stay out of the way. **(PANTOMIME)**

## Shared Writing

**WRITE WELCOMING MESSAGES**

Write on chart paper the words that story characters say that might hurt others' feelings. Read them aloud. Leave space below each sentence for children to help write words of welcome to a friend or sibling, such as *You can come* or *Please play with me.* Encourage children to write the letters for the sounds that they know.

I don't want you tagging along.

Why don't you go play on the swings and stay out of the way?

You'll just mess it up.

Stay away from my castle.

## Repeated Reading

**FOCUS ON PICTURE CLUES**

Share the book again, pausing before reading each page. Ask children to look at the pictures and tell how the expressions on the characters' faces help readers know how the characters are feeling.

**READ AND WRITE INDEPENDENTLY**

**Journal** Place *Jamaica Tag-Along* in the classroom library. Watch and listen to how children tell one another the story as they remember what the characters said and how they felt. Encourage them to write in their Journals about their feelings toward their friends or siblings.

## ☑ Comprehension Check

**ACT IT OUT**

Let children have the opportunity to role-play Jamaica, Ossie, Berto, Berto's mother, and Ossie's friends as you narrate the story. Using facial expressions, children can demonstrate how the characters feel.

**My Read and Write Book, pp. 16–17**

# CENTER WORKSHOPS

## Blocks

### MATERIALS

- Blocks of different sizes and shapes
- Play pieces such as wooden or plastic people and animals
- Natural materials such as acorns, pine cones, and pebbles

## Castle Creations

**Partners** Offer children a variety of cooperative activities and materials to choose from in the Block Center. If you have a sand table, children may choose to work there.

- Give each pair of children a piece of paper that says "We like to build." Children may enjoy drawing a picture of what they have constructed with blocks or other materials and writing about it under their pictures.

- Let children tell the class about their choice of cooperative activity and their unique construction.

*Observation:* Notice which activities children choose and how they work together.

## Music & Movement

### MATERIALS

- Tape recorder
- Audiocassette

## Being Partners

**Partners** Gather children together for a cooperative musical game. Guide children in standing back-to-back with arms locked. Play some music and encourage the pairs to dance while they are connected in this way. When the music stops, everyone can change partners.

If there is an uneven number of children, the extra child can control the music for one round and then join in when the music stops and the partners switch.

*Observation:* How do partners work together to create a dance?

## DAY 5 OBJECTIVES

**CHILDREN WILL:**

- generate rhyming words
- read a rhyme
- review /i/i
- identify words in a sentence
- review high-frequency words
- read My Book: *An Empty Box*
- engage in Center Workshops

## MATERIALS

- *Big Book of Rhymes and Rhythms,* p. 14
- Sentence Strips for "If All the World"
- ABC Card for *Ii*
- *My Read and Write Book,* p. 18
- *My Book: An Empty Box*

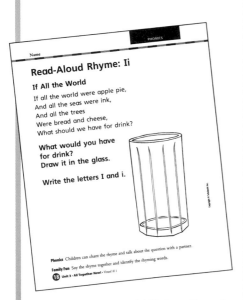

My Read and Write Book, p. 18

For additional practice, see *Scholastic Phonics K,* pp. 51–54. See also Sound and Letter book: *How Many Inches?*

# Sounds and Letters

 DAILY PHONICS

 and Read My Book

## Vowel /i/i

**Ⓐ PHONOLOGICAL AWARENESS**

**Rhyme** Read aloud the rhyme "If All the World" from the *Big Book of Rhymes and Rhythms.* Encourage children to join in as you repeat the rhyme. Ask children to say the words *if* and *ink* slowly, emphasizing the beginning sound.

Say the words *drink* and *ink.* Explain that the sound they hear at the beginning of *if* and *ink* comes in the middle of the word *drink.* Invite children to think of other words that rhyme with *ink* and *drink.*

**Big Book of Rhymes and Rhythms, p. 14**

**Ⓑ CONCEPTS OF PRINT**

Place the *Big Book of Rhymes and Rhythms* in the Reading Center.

- Read "If All the World," asking children to sway from left to right, keeping time to the beat.
- Reread the rhyme. As you read each line, ask volunteers to place the matching Sentence Strip in a pocket chart.
- Remind them that words are separated by spaces. Invite volunteers to frame each word with their fingers.
- Then have children point to the words *if, ink,* and *drink.*

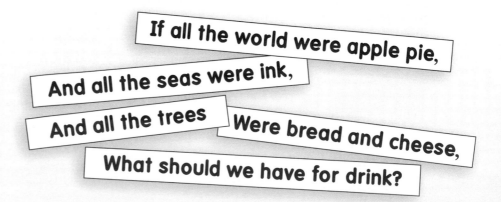

MODIFY Instruction

EXTRA HELP

To reinforce recognition of *Ii*, write children's names that have an *i* that stands for /i/. (Examples: *Will, Kim, Ricky*) Invite children to read the names with you and to point to and highlight every *Ii* they see in the names. (MAKE CONNECTIONS)

C CONNECT SOUND-SPELLING

Alphabetic Principle Remind children that the letter ***i*** stands for /i/ as in ***igloo.*** Flip through the pages of *Eating the Alphabet* and ask children to say "stop" when you get to the ***Ii*** page. Ask children to find the ***Ii*** word on that page. Say the word aloud inviting children to join you.

Point to the ***Ii*** ABC Card and have children name the letter and picture. Explain that the sound /i/ is in the middle of the word *pig.*

ABC Book Explain to children that they are going to make a new page for their own ABC book. Have children make suggestions of words that begin with /i/. When the list is complete, invite children to work together to create an ***Ii*** page for their ABC books.

A Pig Sips Write *A pig sips* on the chalkboard and read it to children as you track the print. Have a volunteer circle the letter *i* in *pig* and *sips*. Then write the words *sits, swims, digs, skips,* and *kicks* and follow the same procedure.

Invite children to draw a picture of the pig sipping through a straw or doing one of the other actions named on the chalkboard. Have children label their drawings and display them to make an *Ii* bulletin board.

D VOCABULARY: HIGH-FREQUENCY WORDS

Write the incomplete sentence ***I see the*** _____ on the chalkboard. Read it aloud and then do the following:

- Review each high-frequency word in the sentence. If necessary, review the read-spell-write routine for each word.
- Write the word ***pig*** in the blank space. Say the word and invite a volunteer to read the new sentence.
- Have children suggest a word that rhymes with *pig* to complete the sentence and repeat the process. Continue with other simple rhyme patterns.

TECHNOLOGY

Let children put *N, S,* and *T* on the **WiggleWorks Plus** Magnet Board. Ask them to add *I* before each letter to make a word that begins with *I.*

The rhyme in the *Big Book of Rhymes and Rhythms* is available on the **Sounds of Phonics** audiocassette.

**An Empty Box**

**ESL/ELD**

▲ As you go through the book again, guide children to notice unusual details by asking questions such as: *What's this?* (a marshmallow) *Can a marshmallow be a flower? Is this a real picture? What's this?* (bread) *Does bread grow in a tree?* (GUIDED QUESTIONS)

# Read My Book

**INTRODUCE THE BOOK**

Let children know that they are going to get their own book that they can read on their own and take home. Talk together about how the bear and the boy had fun together in *Jamberry*.

▶ **Have you ever used your imagination to make a game or a job more fun? What did you do?**

**PREVIEW AND PREDICT**

Pass out copies of *An Empty Box*. Read the title and the author's and illustrator's names. Ask children about the illustration on the cover.

▶ **What are these children doing?**

**READ TOGETHER**

Read the My Book with children, tracking the print as you read. Guide children to point out the different things the boy and girl imagine their box to be.

**PHONICS**

Ask children to say the word *It's* aloud.

▶ **What sound do you hear at the beginning of the word? What letter stands for that sound?**

**READ AND WRITE INDEPENDENTLY**

**Journal** Encourage children to read *An Empty Box* on their own. Provide crayons and invite children to color the illustrations.

**HOME/SCHOOL CONNECTION**

Children can take home their My Books to share with family members and friends. Suggest that children turn a box into something special.

# CENTER WORKSHOPS

**Dramatic Play**

### Act Out *Ii*'s!

Invite children to stand up tall to make a lowercase *i* with their bodies. Children can think of their bodies as the straight line and their heads as the dot.

- Three children can lie on the rug and form a capital letter **I**.

- Children can grow tall "inch by inch." Encourage children to crouch down and see how slowly they can "inch up" to their full height.

- Inchworms are a kind of caterpillar roughly one inch long. Children can inch along the floor as inchworms.

*Observation:* How are children working together to form the letter *Ii*?

#### MATERIALS

- Alphabet Card *Ii*

**Alphabet**

### Form Those *Ii*'s!

Display the Alphabet Card for **Ii**. Invite children to choose the way in which they'd like to form their **Ii**'s!

- Invite children to use paper strips, glue, and buttons to make lowercase *i*'s and to use short and long paper strips to make uppercase *I*'s. Children can paste their uppercase and lowercase *Ii*'s onto colored paper.

- Children may enjoy forming the letters *I* and *i* in sand or with clay.

*Observation:* Notice which children enjoy tactile experiences with letters.

#### MATERIALS

- Alphabet Card *Ii*
- Paper strips
- Glue
- Buttons
- Colored paper
- Sand
- Clay
- Crayons or markers

# Storytelling Circle

## DAY 6 OBJECTIVES

**CHILDREN WILL:**

- recognize /j/
- listen to *The Great Big Enormous Turnip*
- recognize a cumulative story pattern
- discuss problem solving
- recall story sequence
- engage in Center Workshops

## MATERIALS

- Turnip or picture of one
- My Read and Write Book, pp. 19–20

## GUIDED READING

To conclude each day's reading session, meet with guided reading groups. You might use Scholastic's Guided Reading Library or other books in your library.

## Consonant /j/j

### PHONOLOGICAL AWARENESS

**Song** Read aloud the title of the song "John Jacob Jingleheimer Schmidt." Ask children what sound they hear at the beginning of *John, Jacob*, and *Jingleheimer*. Invite children to repeat the words, emphasizing **/j/.**

- Then sing or play the song. Invite children to sing along during a second singing. The verse is usually repeated four times.
- Later, have children clap when they sing words with **/j/.**

> ### John Jacob Jingleheimer Schmidt
> **John Jacob Jingleheimer Schmidt,
> His name is my name, too!
> Whenever we go out,
> The people always shout,
> "There goes John Jacob Jingleheimer Schmidt."
> Da da da da da da da . . .**

## READ Aloud

# The Great Big Enormous Turnip

### A Russian Tale by Alexei Tolstoi

Once upon a time an old man planted a little turnip and said, "Grow, grow, little turnip, grow sweet! Grow, grow, little turnip, grow strong!"

And the turnip grew up sweet and strong and big and enormous.

Then, one day, the old man went to pull it up. He pulled and pulled again, but he could not pull it up.

He called the old woman.

The old woman pulled the old man.

The song is available on the **Sounds of Phonics** audiocassette.

## Build Background

**ORAL LANGUAGE: INVESTIGATE A TURNIP**

Explain that *The Great Big Enormous Turnip* is a Russian folk tale written by Alexei Tolstoi. Pass around an actual turnip or a picture of one. Encourage children to participate in a discussion about the color and shape of the turnip, how it might taste, and the fact that it grows underground.

## Tell the Story

**RECOGNIZE THE STORY PATTERN**

Help children recognize the repetitive pattern by pausing after each new character is added and asking:

▶ **What do you think will happen next?**

Tell or read the story with expression. You might make gestures of straining and pulling at the turnip and give a sigh of relief when it finally comes up at the end.

## Respond to the Literature

**TALK ABOUT IT**

**Share Personal Responses** Invite children to tell what they liked about the story.

▶ **What did you like about the way the people and animals worked together?**

▶ **Did you think that a mouse could make a difference?**

---

The old man pulled the turnip.

And they pulled and pulled again, but they could not pull it up.

So the old woman called her granddaughter.

The granddaughter pulled the old woman.

The old woman pulled the old man.

The old man pulled the turnip.

And they pulled and pulled again, but they could not pull it up.

The granddaughter called the black dog.

The black dog pulled the granddaughter.

The granddaughter pulled the old woman.

The old woman pulled the old man.

The old man pulled the turnip.

And they pulled and pulled again, but they could not pull it up.

The black dog called the cat.

The cat pulled the dog.

The dog pulled the granddaughter.

The granddaughter pulled the old woman.

The old woman pulled the old man.

The old man pulled the turnip.

And they pulled and pulled again, but still they could not pull it up.

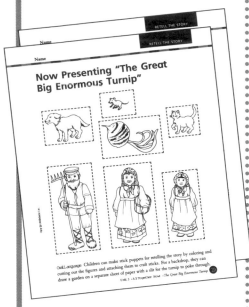

**My Read and Write Book, pp. 19–20**

**THINK ABOUT IT**

**Discuss Story Problem and Solution** Guide children to consider the story problem and resolution.

▶ **What was the problem in this story? How was the problem solved?**

▶ **How would you pull a turnip out of the ground?**

## Shared Writing

**RECORD THE SEQUENCE**

Ask children to recall the order in which the characters are introduced. List the characters' names on a chart. Help children recognize that there is a pattern of size from larger to smaller. Encourage children to draw the characters in a row according to story sequence and to label each character.

## Retell the Story

**CREATE A BOOK**

Retell the story, encouraging children to chime in each time you recite the growing chain of people and animals.

- In groups of six, children can illustrate one of the story scenes.
- Bind the pages together to make a class version of *The Great Big Enormous Turnip*.

## ☑ Comprehension Check

**ACT IT OUT**

Guide children to choose props and pantomime the story as you or another child narrates.

**READ Aloud**

continued from page T81

The cat called the mouse.

The mouse pulled the cat.

The cat pulled the dog.

The dog pulled the granddaughter.

The granddaughter pulled the old woman.

The old woman pulled the old man.

The old man pulled the turnip.

They pulled and pulled again, and up came the turnip at last.

# CENTER WORKSHOPS

## Art

### MATERIALS

- Pieces of yarn or string
- Construction paper
- Crayons, markers, or paints
- Hole punch

## Story Map

Each child can choose a character from *The Great Big Enormous Turnip* and draw that character on construction paper. Make sure every character is chosen by someone.

- Children can cut out the completed characters and punch two holes at the same height on the figure, near the top, one on the right and one on the left.
- Tie a string through the holes and hang the cutouts on a wall or bulletin board.
- Have children place the characters in their order of appearance as they retell the story.
- When finished, emphasize how children worked together to make the story map, just as characters worked together to pull up the turnip.

*Observation:* How do children retell the story with cut-out characters?

## Math 123

### MATERIALS

- Balance scales
- Turnips of different sizes
- Manipulatives such as teddy bear counters

## How Much Could It Weigh?

Place a turnip on one side of a balance scale. Children can place their manipulatives on the other side of the scale to determine how many are equal to the weight of the turnip. Encourage children to estimate how many of their turnips it would take to equal the weight of the great big enormous turnip!

- Children can weigh turnips and talk about which weigh more and which weigh less.
- Provide an assortment of manipulatives for children to use to balance each turnip, letting each child experience the process.

*Observation:* How do children solve the problem of balancing the turnip?

# DAY 7 OBJECTIVES

**CHILDREN WILL:**

- listen for alliteration
- identify **/j/j** and write *Jj*
- talk about the SourceCard
- write directions
- review the high-frequency words
- revisit the High-Frequency Reader: *The Band*
- learn about question marks
- engage in Center Workshops

## MATERIALS

- *Teamwork*, SourceCard 2
- *Jamberry*
- *Jamaica Tag-Along*
- High-Frequency Reader: *The Band*
- My Alphabet Book, p.12

## TECHNOLOGY

 Encourage children to use the drawing and writing tools in the **WiggleWorks Plus** Write area to complete the activities in this lesson.

My Alphabet Book, p. 12

# Read the SourceCard

# Consonant /j/j

### A PHONOLOGICAL AWARENESS

**Alliteration** Read the following alliterative sentence:

*Jack and Jill just joined Jerilyn's jump-rope jamboree.*

Repeat the sentence slowly, emphasizing each **/j/** sound. Ask children to count how many times they hear **/j/.**

### B CONNECT SOUND-SPELLING

**Introduce Consonant /j/j** Show the cover of *Jamberry*. Read the title, emphasizing the **/j/** sound. Repeat the procedure with *Jamaica Tag-Along*. Have a volunteer frame the **J** in each title. Point out that **J** stands for the **/j/** sound in *Jamberry* and *Jamaica*.

- Ask children to say the sound with you.
- If children in the class have names that begin with **/j/,** write them on the chalkboard. Ask the class to say each name, exaggerating the initial **/j/** sound.

## Letter Formation

**WRITE THE LETTER**

Write **Jj** on the chalkboard. Point out the capital and small forms of the letter. Model how to write the letter using the rhymes provided below.

- Have children write both forms of the letter in the air with their fingers. Ask children to make the letter's sound as they practice writing.

### J

**Here's a great big jumping J!**
**Jump right down and bounce away.**
*(Pull down straight. Curve around to the left.)*

### j

**Little *j*'s a fishing hook!**
**Drop it down into the brook.**
*(Pull down straight, into space below base line. Curve around to the left.)*
**Add a dot and take a look.**
*(Add dot.)*

**Side One**

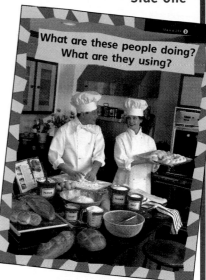

## Share the SourceCard

**SIDE ONE**

**Talk About Cooking** Show children the picture of people working together in a kitchen. Read the questions and invite children's answers.

- Have children point out the cookbook with the recipe, and notice the different ingredients the chefs are using.

- Have them find the labels of the containers—*flour, yeast, sugar,* and *salt.* Read the labels.

- Talk with children about the different cooking tools in the picture, such as the measuring cup, the bowls, and the baking trays.

- Invite discussion about the other things children see in the picture.

**SIDE TWO**

**Read a Recipe** Explain that the recipe on the other side of the SourceCard lists the ingredients, tools, and instructions for making jam sandwiches. Let children know that they will have a chance to follow the recipe.

- Ask volunteers to point to clues that help them understand the recipe.

## Shared Writing

**WRITE DIRECTIONS**

Children can make a poster telling how to make or do something. For example: "How to Feed the Rabbit" or "How to Set a Table." Use side two of the SourceCard as a model.

- Write a title at the top of a chart to tell what the directions are for.

- Fill in the chart as children dictate what belongs in each section. Then read the directions aloud so that children can check to make sure they are complete and in the correct order.

- Invite children to illustrate the "What You Need" and "What You Do" sections of the chart.

**Side Two**

## MODIFY Instruction

### ESL/ELD

▲ Bring in as much realia as possible, including ingredients and tools. Have children act out the process of making jam sandwiches as you read the directions aloud. Practice vocabulary through hands-on activities, such as pointing and picking up objects using the new words. **(USE REALIA)**

**The Band**

## PROFESSIONAL DEVELOPMENT

**GAY SU PINNELL**

### Repeated Readings

*Children need to reread stories many times to develop fluency, gain automaticity with the high-frequency words, have additional blending practice, and develop a sense of comfort in and control over their reading process. As they read the High-Frequency Readers or decodable stories, circulate and take note of those children who need additional help.*

## Revisit High-Frequency Reader

**REREAD THE BOOK**
Invite children to join you as you read the book *The Band* again. On the first page, ask children to read the words that they have already learned. *(Can, you, see,* and *the)* Review these words.

**DECODING STRATEGIES**
As you read the book aloud, point to each word, the initial letter, and the picture clue, pausing long enough for children to read before you do. Model blending as needed. For example, have children use their knowledge of **/g/g** to decode *guitar.*

**Think Aloud** *At the beginning of the word, I see the letter* g. *I know that* g *stands for* **/g/.** *In the picture I see a guitar. The word* guitar *begins with* **/g/.** *This word is* guitar. *That makes sense in the sentence.* (Follow the same steps for *harmonica* and *horn.)*

**CONCEPTS OF PRINT: QUESTION MARKS**
Display the sentence strip for page two and read it aloud. Point out the question mark. Explain that it tells readers that the sentence asks a question.

### Can you see the guitar?

**ORAL LANGUAGE: MUSICAL INSTRUMENTS**
Have children name the musical instruments in the story and then name other instruments they know. Encourage children to discuss which they have heard or played and which they might like to play.

**READ FOR FLUENCY**
Invite children to read *The Band* in a small group. They can pretend to play the instrument named on each page. For the last page, they can each pretend to play a different instrument from the story.

**READ AND WRITE INDEPENDENTLY**
**Journal** Place copies of *The Band* in the Reading Center for children to read on their own. Children can draw or write in their Journals about an instrument they like.

**HOME/SCHOOL CONNECTION**
Children can take home their High-Frequency Reader to share with family members. Together they can talk about a parade that they have seen.

# CENTER WORKSHOPS

**Cooking**

## Making Jam Sandwiches

**Individuals or Partners** Read through the SourceCard recipe with children, checking to see if you have the ingredients, utensils, and implements needed before moving on to the next step. Point out that the recipe has words and pictures.

Guide children to follow the recipe. Have them work individually or in pairs.

To emphasize that we add our own ideas, offer a variety of berry jams for children to choose from.

*Observation:* Notice how children follow the recipe on the SourceCard.

### MATERIALS

- Ingredients, utensils, and implements listed on SourceCard
- Other kinds of berries and berry jams (optional)
- SourceCard 2

**Social Studies**

## Photograph Fun

While the children make the sandwiches in the above activity, take an instant photograph of them carrying out each step listed on side two of the SourceCard.

- Stick a magnet to the back of each photograph and place the photos in an envelope labeled "We make sandwiches!"
- Shuffle the photographs and spread them out on a table. Ask children to place the photographs on the magnetic board to show the order of steps followed to make a sandwich.

*Observation:* Notice how children order the photographs.

### MATERIALS

- Photographs of the children from the cooking activity above
- Envelopes for storing photographs
- Magnets and magnetic board (optional)

# Share the Read Aloud

## DAILY PHONICS

## Consonant /j/j

### Ⓐ PHONOLOGICAL AWARENESS

**Oral Blending** State aloud the following word parts, and ask children to blend them. Provide modeling as needed.

| | | |
|---|---|---|
| /j/ . . . am | /j/ . . . et | /j/ . . . ob |
| /j/ . . . ar | /j/ . . . ack | /j/ . . . eep |

### Ⓑ CONNECT SOUND-SPELLING

**Jeans and Jacket** On chart paper, paste a magazine picture of a child wearing *jeans* and a *jacket,* or draw an outline of jeans and a jacket. Write *jeans* and *jacket* next to the corresponding items, read the words aloud, and circle the letter **j.** Remind children that the letter **j** stands for **/j/.** Invite children to suggest words that begin with **/j/.** Write each word on the chart paper, and have volunteers circle the letter **j.** Invite children to illustrate some of the words.

**My Read and Write Book,** p. 21

## Build Background

**ORAL LANGUAGE: PUTTING ON A PLAY**

Invite children to talk about times they have participated in or seen a play. Guide children to understand that a play is a story that is acted out in front of an audience. Discuss performance words such as *audience, clap, bow,* and *act.*

**PREVIEW AND PREDICT**

Show children the cover of the book, reading the title and the author/illustrator's name as you track the print.

- Explain that *The Story of Chicken Licken* is based on an old folk tale, and that it is also known as *Henny Penny* or *Chicken Little.*
- Encourage children to talk about the title page. Where do they think the story takes place?

**SET A PURPOSE**

Invite children to look for ways that this version of the story is different from others they might know.

## Share the Read Aloud

**CHARACTERS AND SPEECH BUBBLES**

As you read *The Story of Chicken Licken*, check that children understand that the speech bubbles show the words that a character is saying. Be sure children understand which characters are speaking which words. Encourage children to:

• point to the character who is speaking.

• notice how sentences are repeated.

• listen for rhyming names.

The Story of Chicken Licken

## Respond to the Literature

**TALK ABOUT IT**

**Share Personal Responses** Ask children if they liked *The Story of Chicken Licken*. Encourage them to share their favorite parts of the story.

▶ Have you heard this story before?

▶ Was there anything you wondered about or found confusing in this version of *Chicken Licken*?

▶ What happens in the audience?

**THINK ABOUT IT**

**Talk About Thinking for Yourself** Invite children to discuss how important it is to think for yourself.

▶ Why did Chicken Licken think the sky had fallen?

▶ Would you have believed Chicken Licken the way the animals did? What would you say or do if someone told you the sky had fallen?

▶ Who else did the animals believe at the end of the story?

▶ What might have happened if they hadn't believed Foxy Woxy?

**MODIFY Instruction**

**GIFTED & TALENTED**

※ As a follow-up activity, ask children to change some of the dialogue in the story. Read the book page by page, inviting children to innovate and add some of their own words the way they would speak. How different is the revised story? **(INNOVATE)**

## MODIFY
Instruction

### ESL/ELD

▲ Review the concept of rhyming words before the Shared Writing activity. Provide extra practice for English language learners by saying two words at a time. Encourage children to listen and decide if the words rhyme. **(USE RHYME)**

## Shared Writing

**CREATE RHYMING ANIMAL NAMES**

Children will enjoy making up rhyming animal names.

• Ask children to recall some of the rhyming names from the story—*Chicken Licken, Henny Penny, Cock Lock, Duck Luck, Drake Lake, Goose Loose, Gander Lander, Turkey Lurkey,* and *Foxy Woxy.*

• Invite children to make up rhyming names for other animals. Write the names on strips of oaktag for children to illustrate.

## Repeated Reading

**FOCUS ON PLOT**

Point out that while the children's play tells a story about Chicken Licken, the pictures of the audience tell another story. Invite children to use the pictures to tell the story of the baby in the audience. On each page, ask volunteers to tell what is happening on stage and in the audience.

**READ AND WRITE INDEPENDENTLY**

**Journal** Place *The Story of Chicken Licken* in the Reading Center so that children can read it on their own. Invite children to write favorite animal names in their Journals. They may wish to draw pictures of animals to go with the names.

## ✅ Comprehension Check

**ACT IT OUT**

Narrate the story and invite children to take the parts of the nine animals—chicken, hen, cock, duck, drake, goose, gander, turkey, and fox. Remaining children can play the audience members, including the toddler, the mother, and the baby.

• Help children make tags to wear around their necks, with the name of the character they are playing. Animal characters may enjoy using masks like those they make in the Center Workshop, or you may want to have children use face paints.

• Remind children to speak their part loudly and clearly.

• After the performance, applaud the children for each having an important part in retelling the story.

# CENTER WORKSHOPS

### Art

## MATERIALS

- **Paper plates and craft sticks**
- **Glue or paste**
- **Scissors**
- **Crayons or markers**
- **Construction paper**
- **Yarn, buttons, beads, feathers, glitter**

## Make Animal Faces!

**Individuals** Invite children to make masks for the different characters in the story.

- Children can make simple masks from paper plates and craft sticks. They can draw faces on the plates, or glue on buttons or beads for features.

- Beaks can be formed out of construction paper and glued on. Feathers would make another fun addition to the masks. Glue a craft stick to the bottom of each mask. Children can hold it in front of their face.

*Observation:* How do children create masks for their play?

### Alphabet

## MATERIALS

- **Just the children**

## Fowl Play

Many games are based on animals that are in *The Story of Chicken Licken*. Children may enjoy a round of "Duck, Duck, Goose." Here's another game they will enjoy:

- **Hawks and Hens** This game from Zimbabwe calls for at least four players and two safety zones. One child is the hawk. All the other children are hens. The hens run back and forth between the safety zones while the hawk stands in the middle, trying to catch them. Hens that are caught must sit to the side. The last hen to be caught becomes the next hawk, and the game begins again.

*Observation:* Notice which children particularly like active games.

## DAY 9 OBJECTIVES

**CHILDREN WILL:**

- orally segment words (beginning sound)
- read a rhyme
- review /j/j
- connect speaking and writing
- review high-frequency words
- read My Book: *Our Snowman*
- engage in Center Workshops

## MATERIALS

- *Big Book of Rhymes and Rhythms,* p. 15
- Sentence Strips for "Jack Be Nimble"
- *Jamberry*
- High-Frequency Reader: *The Band*
- My Book: *Our Snowman*
- My Read and Write Book, p. 22

**Read-Aloud Rhyme: Jj**

Jack

Jack be nimble,
Jack be quick,
Jack jump over
The candlestick.

Draw a picture of yourself jumping.

Write the letters J and j.

**Phonics** After chanting the rhyme, children can draw a picture of themselves jumping.
**Family Fun** Say the rhyme together. Ask your child to act it out.
Unit 3 · All Together Now! · Consonant *j* j

**My Read and Write Book, p. 22**

For additional practice see *Scholastic Phonics K,* pp. 55–58. See also Sound and Letter book: *Jump!*

# Sounds and Letters

## Consonant /j/j

**A** **PHONOLOGICAL AWARENESS**

**Oral Segmentation: Beginning Sounds**
Read aloud "Jack Be Nimble" from the *Big Book of Rhymes and Rhythms*. Then invite children to recite it along with you.

Ask children what sound they hear at the beginning of the words *Jack* and *jump*. Ask them to say *Jack* and *jump* slowly, isolating the beginning sound: *j-j-jack, j-j-jump*. Encourage children to name other words that begin with **/j/**.

**Big Book of Rhymes and Rhythms, p. 15**

**B** **CONCEPTS OF PRINT**

Place the *Big Book of Rhymes and Rhythms,* the Sentence Strips for "Jack Be Nimble," and a pocket chart in the Reading Center. Then do the following:

- Recite "Jack Be Nimble" with children as you track the words. Ask them to jump when you get to the word *jump*.
- Let a child place the Sentence Strips in the pocket chart as the group recites each line. Invite children to count the number of words in each line.
- Ask a volunteer to point to a name or word that begins with the letter *Jj* each time the word is said.

Jack be nimble,

Jack be quick,

Jack jump over

The candlestick.

## MODIFY
### Instruction

## EXTRA HELP

■ To reinforce the connection between the letter *Jj* and its sound, display a variety of labeled objects whose names begin with *Jj*, such as jellybeans, a jar, a jacket, a toy jet, jacks, and a jump rope. Ask children to repeat the name for each object. **(USE REALIA)**

## Ⓒ CONNECT SOUND-SPELLING

**Alphabetic Principle** Distribute Little Book copies of *Jamberry*. Ask children to frame the letter *J* in *Jamberry* and read the title. Remind children that the letter *j* stands for **/j/.** Invite them to turn the pages to find additional words that begin with *Jj*. *(jamberry, jam, jamble, jazzberry, jamming, jamboree)*

**ABC Book** Explain to children that they are going to make a new page for their own ABC book. Have children suggest animals, objects, and people whose names begin with **/j/.**

If they suggest **/j/** words that begin with the letter *Gg*, tell them that the sound is the same, but that in some words *Gg* stands for **/j/.** When the list of *j* words is complete, invite children to work together to create the *Jj* page for their ABC books.

**Jump** Read the directions aloud. After children perform each action, have them repeat the word in the direction that begins with **/j/.** Write it on the chalkboard and read it aloud. Have a volunteer frame the letter *Jj*.

- Jump up and down.
- Point to your jaw.
- Pretend to juggle.
- Jog in place.

## Ⓓ VOCABULARY: HIGH-FREQUENCY WORDS

Write the incomplete sentence *Can you see the _____ ?* on the chalkboard. Then do the following:

- Review the high-frequency words *can, you, see,* and *the.* If necessary, review the read-spell-write routine.

- Read aloud *The Band.* Ask a volunteer to complete the sentence stem with something they see on each page.

- Write each new sentence on the chalkboard and invite children to read it.

## TECHNOLOGY

Children can write the word *jumps* on the **WiggleWorks Plus** Magnet Board. Help children copy the word and add their own and other names to make sentences.

The rhyme in the *Big Book of Rhymes and Rhythms* is available on the **Sounds of Phonics** audiocassette.

**Our Snowman**

ESL/ELD

▲ Place sticky notes over the last word or words in each sentence that follow, *We give him . . .* Encourage English language learners to use picture clues to help them provide the missing words. Ask them to pronounce each new word, and make sure the child knows its meaning by asking which picture helped him/her. **(CLOZE)**

# Read My Book

**INTRODUCE THE BOOK**

Let children know that they are going to get their own book that they can read on their own and take home.

▶ **When you work on a project with other children, does everyone's idea always get used?**

**PREVIEW AND PREDICT**

Pass out copies of *Our Snowman*. Read the title and the author's and illustrator's names. Talk about the cover illustration.

▶ **What are these children doing?**

▶ **What might this book be about?**

**READ TOGETHER**

Read the My Book with children, tracking the print as you read. Encourage children to think of a name for the snowman and to write it on the last page of the book.

**PHONICS**

Ask children to say the word *hat* aloud.

▶ **What sound do you hear at the beginning of the word? What letter stands for that sound?**

**READ AND WRITE INDEPENDENTLY**

**Journal** Encourage children to read *Our Snowman* on their own or in small groups. Provide crayons and invite children to color the illustrations. They may wish to create their own snowman picture and write about it in their Journals.

**HOME/SCHOOL CONNECTION**

Children can take home their My Book to share with family members. They can make a collaborative drawing in which they take turns adding details to a snowman, house, farm, or other picture of their choice.

# CENTER WORKSHOPS

## Games

### MATERIALS

- Jump ropes
- Jacks
- Cards with pictures of *Jj* words

## Play with *Jj*!

Play a *Jj* guessing game. Children can pick a card from the stack and give clues to each picture name: "I'm thinking of a *Jj* word that names something you wear." (*jeans, jumper, jacket*)

- Invite children to play jump rope as they recite jump-rope rhymes that feature lots of *Jj* words.
- Children can act out nursery rhymes that feature characters whose names begin with J. ("Jack and Jill," "Jack Spratt," "Little Jack Horner")
- Although most children will not have the fine-motor skills needed for jacks, you might demonstrate the game and let children try it.

*Observation:* Listen for the *Jj* words children use as they play the games.

Little Jumping Joan
Here I am,
Little Jumping Joan.
When nobody's with me,
I'm all alone.

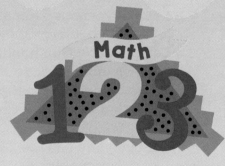

## Math

### MATERIALS

- Variety of juices
- Mini-sized paper cups

## Judging Juice!

Invite children to taste several different juices, such as apple, orange, and grape.

Provide a simple graph labeled with the name of each kind of juice. Give children colored stickers and ask them to write their names. Then invite them to place their sticker beneath the name of their favorite juice.

When the judges are finished, talk about the graph. Encourage children to make comparison statements.

*Observation:* How do children compare the juices? Listen for comparative statements.

## DAY 10 OBJECTIVES

## DAY 10 OBJECTIVES

**CHILDREN WILL:**

- respond to song through movement
- compare and contrast the books they've shared
- participate in writing a group chart
- maintain /i/i and /j/j
- illustrate rhyming words
- create a final project

## MATERIALS

- *Jamberry*
- *Jamaica Tag-Along*
- *The Story of Chicken Licken*

## TECHNOLOGY

 Encourage children to use the drawing and writing tools in the **WiggleWorks Plus** Write area to complete the project and activities.

For more computer activities, see the Technology Teaching Plan.

# Put It All Together

## Sum It Up

**TALK ABOUT WORKING TOGETHER**

Remind children that they have been reading and talking about characters who work together and share ideas. Encourage children to talk about situations where they worked with others to get something done and how they shared their ideas.

**ORAL LANGUAGE: SONG**

Sing "Let Everyone Clap Hands Like Me" inviting children to sing along and carry out the motions. Afterward, ask children if they had fun doing the same things together.

▶ **Do we all clap, sneeze, yawn, jump, and laugh in exactly the same way, or do we all have our own ways of doing things?**

Explore this idea by inviting children to demonstrate various actions. Encourage them to compare and discuss the differences and similarities in the ways the actions were performed.

### Let Everyone Clap Hands Like Me

Let everyone clap hands like me.
   (clap, clap)
Let everyone clap hands like me.
   (clap, clap)
Come on and join in the game.
You'll find that it's always the same.
   (clap, clap)
Let everyone sneeze like me.
   (kerchoo!)
Let everyone yawn like me.
   (yawn)
Let everyone jump up like me.
   (jump)
Let everyone laugh like me.
   (ha-ha)

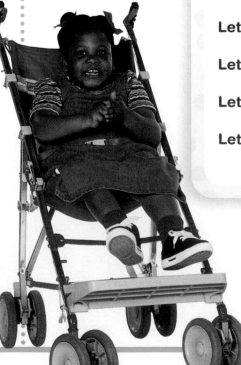

## Language Experience Chart

**COMPARE AND CONTRAST CHART**

Display the books that children have read during the previous nine days. Talk together about the books and the folk tale children shared. Respond to any questions children may have.

- Make a language chart entitled "We Add Our Own Ideas." Talk together about how this theme applies to each of the stories children have read together. Write children's responses on the language chart, which might look like the one shown.

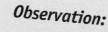

**We Add Our Own Ideas**

| Jamberry | Jamaica Tag-Along | The Great Big Enormous Turnip | The Story of Chicken Licken |
|---|---|---|---|
| A boy and a bear have a wonderful time as they find unique ways to pick and eat all kinds of berries. | Jamaica figures out how to get along with others. | Only after all of the characters helped did the turnip finally come out of the ground. | A cast of children work together to act out an old tale in a new way. |

**Observation:**

How are children doing? Are they:
- writing about their favorite stories?
- recognizing how the stories relate to the theme?
- recalling story details?
- talking about books?

**MODIFY Instruction**

### ESL/ELD

▲ Help children recall and summarize the books by having them tell you which word is missing from each of the following sentence stems:
*My favorite story is _____.*
*My favorite animal is _____.*
Then have them brainstorm new words they remember from all the stories while the teacher writes them on a list. **(KEY WORDS)**

**EXTRA HELP**

■ Help children recognize the **/j/** sound by asking them to focus on the position of their mouth, lips, and tongue as they say each word aloud. **(DEMONSTRATE)**

DAILY PHONICS

# Maintenance

## Ⓐ PHONOLOGICAL AWARENESS

**Picture Rhyme** Say aloud the following sets of words. Have children identify which two rhyme. Use picture cards if available.

pig, pen, wig     lid, dog, log     jar, jet, car

Have children fold a piece of paper in half. Ask them to draw pictures of two things whose names rhyme, one on each half of their paper. Children may use the examples you have provided or any rhyming words they choose.

## Ⓑ PHONICS ACTIVITY

**Pack June's Jeep** At the top of chart paper write the following heading and read it to children:
**Help June Pack Her Jeep.**

- Have children point to the letter *Jj* at the beginning of *June* and *jeep* and say the sound it stands for.

- Then tell children that June is going on a long trip in her jeep.

- Invite them to name things that begin with the sound **/j/** that June might pack in her jeep. *(jump rope, jacks, jar of jam, jug of juice, jacket, jeans)*

- List children's suggestions in a column on the chart. When they have finished, read the items in the list and invite children to illustrate them.

# WEEKS 3 AND 4
# PROJECT

# "Big Book of Recipes"

In Weeks 3 and 4, children have explored the ways that people work together and still add their own ideas. For the unit project, children can work together to create a "Big Book of Recipes."

Tell children that they are going to work together to make a big book of recipes. To prepare for this activity, ask them to bring in a favorite recipe from home.

Write each recipe children bring in on a separate sheet of chart paper. Read each one together. Then encourage children to talk about their own favorite recipes. They can name a favorite food and describe what they think is in it and how they think it is made. Write each child's favorite recipe on a separate sheet of chart paper.

## MATERIALS

- **Family recipes**
- **Chart paper**
- **Crayons**

## BENCHMARKS

**Monitor children's progress. Are they**

- working together and helping one another?

- participating in discussing foods they like?

- extending the idea of teamwork to a new experience?

Work with children to sort the recipes into breakfast, lunch, dinner, and snack categories. Challenge children to point out the foods that fit into more than one category.

Guide children to form five groups. Give four of the groups the recipes for the meals that belong to one of the categories, and invite them to illustrate each recipe. Then each group can design and illustrate a page with the title "Breakfast Recipes," "Lunch Recipes," "Dinner Recipes," or "Snack Recipes" to place in front of their section of recipes. The fifth group can design a cover with the title "Big Book of Recipes." Let all of the children write their names on the cover as the authors and illustrators. Bind the pages of the book and place it where children have easy access to it.

Help children write a letter to their families, inviting them to attend a family pot luck get-together at the end of the sixth week. Ask each family to bring one of their favorite dishes to share. Mention in the letter that the children's "Big Book of Recipes" will be on display for all to enjoy.

# WEEKS
# 5 AND 6

# Kindergarten Goals
## for Weeks 5 and 6

## Oral Language/ Vocabulary

- participating in group discussions
- participating in choral reading, songs, poems
- building vocabulary about cooking, plants, numbers, colors
- discussing the culture of others
- exploring story vocabulary

## Reading

- building alphabetic knowledge
- participating actively in shared reading
- engaging in emergent reading
- exploring concepts of print
- recognizing story sequence
- using picture clues to predict text
- identifying action words
- recognizing story patterns
- reading high-frequency words

## Writing

- making a food ABC book
- writing captions
- writing letters: *Kk, Ll*
- writing words, sentences, questions
- writing answers to questions
- writing a language-experience chart
- creating a menu
- engaging in shared writing
- writing independently in Journals

## Listening/Speaking/ Viewing

- listening to read alouds
- exploring rhyme and rhythm
- developing phonological awareness
- listening to check predictions
- listening to gain knowledge of other cultures
- retelling a story in their own words
- dramatizing a story
- engaging in conversations
- sharing personal experiences
- comparing stories
- demonstrating visual literacy

## Daily Phonics: *Kk* and *Ll*

- reciting classic poems, songs, and nursery rhymes
- naming and recognizing the letters
- recognizing sound/letter relationships
- generating words with /k/, /l/
- decoding words using /k/k, /l/l

## Center Workshops and Project

- acquiring world knowledge through cross-curricular activities
- making a "Big Book of Menus" and hosting a family get-together

# WEEKS 5 AND 6 RESOURCES

## Big Book

**Meet the Author**

Grace Maccarone loves books! Besides writing, she edits books for Scholastic.

**Meet the Illustrator**

Emily Arnold McCully won the Caldecott Medal for *Mirette on the High Wire*.

Available as audiocassette

## Big Book of Rhymes and Rhythms

For teaching phonological awareness, the alphabet, and concepts of print.

- "Humpty Dumpty"
- "Mary Had a Little Lamb"

Available as audiocassette

## Read Aloud

**Meet the Author/ Illustrator**

Robert McCloskey's career was first launched when, as a high school student, he entered Scholastic Magazine's annual Art Award Contest and won an art school scholarship. Little Sal in this story was based on his own daughter, Sally.

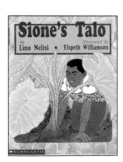

## Read Aloud

**Meet the Author**

Lino Nelisi has taught elementary school in her native Niue and in Auckland. She decided to become a children's writer when she discovered how few books there were about life in the Pacific Islands.

## ABC Book

**Meet the Author/Illustrator**

For this book, Lois Ehlert bought apples, apricots, artichokes, asparagus, and an avocado to use as models for paintings. It took her a whole year before she finally bought zucchini!

**Side One**

**Side Two**

## SourceCard

- What fruits and vegetables do you see?
- "Jamboree" by David McCord

## High-Frequency Reader

**My Read and Write Book**

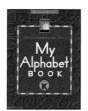

**My Alphabet Book**

**ESL/ELD Teaching Guide**

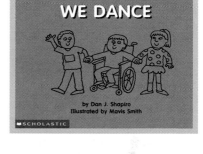

## My Books

**To take home to share.**

# Introducing the Mentor

Children in the neighborhood enjoy visiting Two Boots because Kawku Twumasi shares his work with them. He can often be seen in the window making pizza. When children sit in the restaurant, they are invited to draw on their placemats.

# DAYS AT A GLANCE

## WEEKS 5 AND 6

| | Daily Phonics | Literature | Shared Writing | Workshops and Projects |
|---|---|---|---|---|
| **DAY 1** | Phonological Awareness: Auditory Discrimination<br><br>Review /h/h, /i/i, /j/j | *Eating the Alphabet* by Lois Ehlert | Make a Food ABC Book | Math: Fruit Graph<br><br>Art: Fruit and Vegetable Collage |
| **DAY 2** | **Consonant /k/k**<br>Phonological Awareness: Oral Segmentation | *Pizza Party!* by Grace Maccarone illustrated by Emily Arnold McCully | Focus on Sentences | Art: Draw It!<br><br>Art: Play-Dough Delight |
| **DAY 3** | **Consonant /k/k**<br>Phonological Awareness: Alliteration<br><br>Introduce Sound-Spelling | *Pizza Party!* by Grace Maccarone<br><br>**High-Frequency Reader:** *We Are Painting* | Concepts of Print: Words<br><br>Write *Kk*<br><br>Make a Class Book | Writing: Tell a Story<br><br>Cooking: Our Own Pizza Party! |
| **DAY 4** | **Consonant /k/k**<br>Phonological Awareness: Oral Blending<br><br>Review Sound-Spelling | *Blueberries for Sal* by Robert McCloskey | Writing Sentences | Art: Melted Crayon Art<br><br>Cooking: A "Berry Good Smoothie!" |
| **DAY 5** | **Consonant /k/k**<br>Phonological Awareness: Rhyme<br><br>Maintain Sound-Spelling | "Humpty Dumpty" a rhyme<br><br>*Eating the Alphabet*<br><br>**My Book:** *We Dance* | Concepts of Print: Word Boundaries and Punctuation<br><br>High-Frequency Words: *we, are* | Cooking: Kiwi Kabobs!<br><br>Art: Kites of *Kk* |

| | Daily Phonics | Literature | Shared Writing | Workshops and Projects |
|---|---|---|---|---|
| **DAY 6** | Consonant /l/l<br>Phonological Awareness:<br>Oral Segmentation | *Pizza*<br>by Saturnino<br>Romay | Create a Menu | Math: Equal Parts<br><br>Dramatic Play:<br>Pizza Parlor |
| **DAY 7** | Consonant /l/l<br>Phonological Awareness:<br>Alliteration<br><br>Introduce Sound-<br>Spelling | SourceCard<br>What Do You See?<br>"Jamboree"<br><br>**High-Frequency Reader:**<br>*We Are Painting* | Answer a Question<br>Write *Ll* | Writing: A Picture<br>Rhyming Book<br><br>Dramatic Play:  Our<br>Fruit and Vegetable<br>Stand |
| **DAY 8** | Consonant /l/l<br>Phonological Awareness:<br>Oral Blending<br><br>Review Sound-Spelling | *Sione's Talo*<br>by Lino Nelisi<br>illustrated by<br>Elspeth Williamson<br><br>READ ALOUD | Write Repeated<br>Phrases | Science: Taking<br>Root<br><br>Science: Observe an<br>Ant Colony |
| **DAY 9** | Consonant /l/l<br>Phonological Awareness:<br>Rhyme<br><br>Maintain Sound-Spelling | "Mary Had a Little Lamb"<br>a nursery rhyme<br>*Eating the Alphabet*<br>**My Book:** *I Read, You Read* | Concepts of Print:<br>Develop Print<br>Awareness<br><br>High-Frequency<br>Words | Math: Lids! Lids!<br>Lids!<br><br>Art: Looking at<br>Leaves |
| **DAY 10** | Mid-year Review | **Review Books from<br>Weeks 5 and 6** | Make a Compare<br>and Contrast Chart | Project: "Big Book<br>of Menus" |

## DAY 1 OBJECTIVES

**CHILDREN WILL:**

- develop phonological awareness
- review /h/h, /i/i, /j/j
- discuss describing words
- read and respond to *Eating the Alphabet*
- build alphabetic knowledge
- write a group ABC Book
- engage in Center Workshops

## MATERIALS

- *Eating the Alphabet*

## GUIDED READING

To conclude each day's reading session, meet with guided reading groups. You might use Scholastic's Guided Reading Library or other books in your library.

# Share the ABC Book

## Warm-Up: Word Play

### A PHONOLOGICAL AWARENESS

Sing the song "Apples and Bananas" with children. Draw attention to how the words *apples* and *bananas* change in each verse.

### Apples and Bananas

I like to eat, eat, eat
I like to eat apples and bananas
I like to eat, eat, eat
I like to eat apples and bananas

2. I like to ate…ayples and banaynays

3. I like to eet…eeples and banenees

4. I like to ite…iples and baninis

5. I like to ote…oples and banonos

6. I like to ute…uples and banunus

### B PHONICS MAINTENANCE

**Letters /h/h, /i/i, /j/j** Find or make picture cards for the following words: *hammer, house, horse, hat, ink, insect, igloo, jacket, juggle, jar.* Then write the letters **h, i,** and **j** in columns on chart paper. Ask children to place the picture cards in the appropriate columns.

## Build Background

**ORAL LANGUAGE: DESCRIBING WORDS**

Put familiar fruits and vegetables in a bag. Ask a volunteer to close his or her eyes and pull one out.

▶ **How does it feel? How does it smell? What is it?**

Make a list of the describing words.

**PREVIEW AND PREDICT**

Invite volunteers to introduce *Eating the Alphabet*.

▶ **What kind of book is this? What is inside?**

# Read the ABC Book

**ALPHABETIC KNOWLEDGE: *Kk* AND *Ll***

Read *Eating the Alphabet* in one sitting. While you read, encourage children to:

- point out things in the illustrations, naming the fruits and vegetables.
- notice that the fruits and vegetables are listed alphabetically by the first letters in their names.
- guess the names of fruits and vegetables that are unfamiliar to them.

Stop on the pages for *Kk* and *Ll.* Point out the uppercase and lowercase letters. Say the names of the fruits and vegetables, emphasizing the beginning sounds.

**Eating the Alphabet**

# Respond to the Literature

**TALK ABOUT IT**

**Share Personal Responses** Talk with children about the fruits and vegetables in the ABC book.

▶ **Which fruits and vegetables have you seen or eaten? Have you ever seen a *star fruit* or a *quince*?**

Model how to use the glossary in the back of the book to find out where the different fruits and vegetables grow.

**THINK ABOUT IT**

**Ideas for Good Nutrition** Talk about fruits and vegetables children like to eat. Ask children about the different ways they have eaten fruits and vegetables. Have they eaten vegetables raw? How about cooked?

- If possible, refer to a food guide pyramid. Talk about the number of fruits and vegetables we should eat each day.
- Ask which fruits and vegetables children eat every day.
- Make a chart with three columns: *Breakfast, Lunch,* and *Dinner.*
- Invite children to suggest healthy foods that might go under each column.

**MODIFY Instruction**

## EXTRA HELP

■ Whenever possible, allow children—especially visually impaired children or kinesthetic learners—an opportunity to handle the objects before or after you describe them to give hands-on, sensory experience. **(MULTISENSORY TECHNIQUES)**

## MODIFY Instruction

### ESL/ELD

▲ After children talk about the different ways that they have eaten fruits and vegetables, invite English language learners to choose a fruit or vegetable and make a drawing that shows how they like to eat it. They may want to add information from the glossary with the assistance of an English-speaking partner. **(WORK IN PAIRS)**

## Shared Writing

**FOOD ABC BOOK**

Work together to make a food ABC book. Write **Aa is for _____** on a piece of chart paper, and invite children to suggest foods that begin with the letter *Aa*. Invite children to complete the sentence by writing in their ideas.

• Let children offer ideas for each letter, completing the ABC book in one sitting or over the course of a few sittings.

• Let children illustrate the ABC book with drawings or cutouts of different foods. When you get to *Zz,* staple the pages together, and write "Our Yummy ABC Book." Invite children to write their names on the cover.

**WRITE A NOTE**

Invite a volunteer to write a note that says, "Read our ABC Book." Post the note where classroom visitors can see it.

## Repeated Reading

**LETTERS AND SOUNDS**

Reread the ABC book, paying particular attention to the *Kk* and *Ll* pages.

• Point out the highlighted letters on each page.

• Talk about pages that have words that start with the same letter but have a different sound. *(C: corn, celery; O: okra, onion)*

• Point out that the letters and words are written twice, once in capital letters and once in lowercase letters. Turn the book to show children the words that are printed sideways.

**READ AND WRITE INDEPENDENTLY**

**Journal** Encourage children to read *Eating the Alphabet* on their own or in small groups. Children can write in their Journals about interesting names for fruits and vegetables.

## ✓ Comprehension Check

**ACT IT OUT**

Children can act out situations using fruits and vegetables. For example, children can pretend to shop for, cook, and eat different foods. Guide children to think of props they can use, such as a shopping list, recipe, pictures of foods, and supermarket flyers.

# CENTER WORKSHOPS

**Math 123**

## MATERIALS

- **Photograph of each child**
- **Blocks or milk cartons**
- **Pictures of fruits and vegetables**
- **Tape**
- **Butcher paper**

## Fruit Graph

Create reusable graph blocks for each child by taping a photograph of him or her to a block. You can also use milk cartons by cutting off the top and taping the photographs to the sides of the cartons. Label with children's first names.

- Tape to the wall a large piece of paper with pictures of different fruits across the top.
- Encourage children to place their graph block below the fruit that they like best.
- Discuss which fruit is the group's favorite.
- Guide children to count how many people chose each fruit or vegetable and to label it with that number.

*Observation:* Notice how children count and compare who chose each fruit.

**Art**

## MATERIALS

- **Magazines**
- **Colorful supermarket flyers**
- **Seed catalogs and/or catering brochures**
- **Scissors**
- **Butcher paper**
- **Glue**

## Fruit and Vegetable Collage

Children can work together to make a fruit and vegetable collage.

- Encourage children to find and cut out pictures of fruits and vegetables. Children can glue the pictures to a large sheet of butcher paper placed on the floor.
- Label the names of the fruits and vegetables. Let children write other information about each fruit or vegetable, such as its shape and color.

Hang the finished collage on a wall.

*Observation:* How do children work together to make a group collage?

tomatoes
melons

## DAY 2 OBJECTIVES

**CHILDREN WILL:**

- recognize /k/
- listen and respond to *Pizza Party!*
- focus on rhythm and rhyme
- recognize word and sentence boundaries
- engage in Center Workshops

## MATERIALS

- *Pizza Party!*
- **My Read and Write Book,** p. 23

The Big Book is available on audiocassette in the Literacy Place Listening Center.

The song is available in the **Sounds of Phonics** audiocassette.

**My Read and Write Book,** p. 23

# Share the Big Book

## Consonant /k/k

### PHONOLOGICAL AWARENESS

**Oral Segmentation: Beginning Sounds** Read aloud the title of the song, "Kookaburra."

- Invite children to say the word *Kookaburra*, isolating the beginning sound: *k-k-kookaburra.*
- Then sing or play the song. Invite children to sing along during a second singing.
- During later singings, have children clap each time they hear a word that begins with **/k/.**

### Kookaburra

Kookaburra sits in the old gum tree
Merry merry king of the bush is he
Laugh Kookaburra, laugh Kookaburra
Gay your life must be
Kookaburra sits in the old gum tree
Eating all the gumdrops he can see
Stop Kookaburra, stop Kookaburra
Leave some there for me

## Build Background

**ORAL LANGUAGE: COOKING**

Invite children to talk about cooking. If possible, bring in various cooking utensils and discuss how each is used.

▶ **Have you helped cook? How?**

**PREVIEW AND PREDICT**

Show children the cover of the book. Read the title and the author's and illustrator's names. Encourage children to talk about the cover illustration.

▶ **What are the people on the cover doing?**

**SET A PURPOSE**

Ask children what they think this book might be about. Write down their ideas and invite them to listen to find out.

## Read the Big Book

**LISTEN TO THE RHYTHM AND RHYME**

Read the book. Emphasize the pattern of rhythm and rhyme by reading with a lilting voice and having fun. Stop after page 5 and ask:

▶ **Which words rhyme with *fill*?**

▶ **How many words rhyme with *pour*?**

Then ask children to listen for more words that rhyme as you continue to read. Encourage children to look for picture clues to help them complete the rhymes.

## Respond to the Literature

**TALK ABOUT IT**

**Share Personal Responses** Let children talk about the parts of the book they particularly liked.

▶ **What did you like about the book? What did you not like?**

▶ **What happened in the book? Were you surprised by anything?**

**THINK ABOUT IT**

**Working Together** Talk about what the children in the book did. Point out that the author uses the word *we*.

▶ **Why do you think the author used the word *we* instead of the word *I*?**

▶ **Did the children in the book work together, or did they work on their own?**

▶ **How are the characters in *Pizza Party!* like those in *Tortillas*?**

Encourage children to talk about a time when they have worked together.

▶ **Have you ever helped cook at home?**

▶ **Did working together make the task easier or harder? Did it make it more fun?**

**Pizza Party!**

**MODIFY Instruction**

**EXTRA HELP**

▪ To review vocabulary and word meaning, encourage children to pantomime activities from the story. You might make up word cards for some of the story words. Invite children to take turns choosing cards. Together, say each word and have the child act out the word or an activity related to it. **(PANTOMIME)**

# ☀ DAY 2

## OBSERVATION

How are children doing?
Are they:

- recognizing the repetitive use of "We . . ." throughout the book?

- noticing how the children in the book are cooperating and helping one another?

- able to connect the book to their own experiences?

## PROFESSIONAL DEVELOPMENT

**GAY SU PINNELL**

*Using the Word Wall*

*The Word Wall should not be a decoration; it should be a valuable reference tool for children. Make children accountable for the words on the Wall as they read and write. During writing, have children refer to the Wall for help. In addition, you can also use Word Wall words as key words when "sharing the pen" during Interactive Writing.*

## Shared Writing

**FOCUS ON SENTENCES**

Show children the sentence "We taste." in *Pizza Party!* Write it on the chalkboard in large print. Point out the period and remind children that it tells us that "We taste." is a sentence. Ask children to use their index fingers to write the word *We* on the floor. Point out the capital letter at the beginning of the word. Talk with children about the words on the chart:

▶ **How many letters do you see in the word *We*?**

▶ **What do you see between the words?**

Then reread the sentence "We taste." Let children tell you what the period means. Children can illustrate the chart and act out the sentence by pretending to taste different things.

## Repeated Reading

**USE PICTURE CLUES TO PREDICT TEXT**

Reread the Big Book with children. As you read:

- encourage children to look for clues in the pictures and to think about what the children in the pictures are doing.

- guide children to chime in as you read the word *we*, and to predict what words might follow.

**READ AND WRITE INDEPENDENTLY**

**Journal** Place copies of *Pizza Party!* in the Reading Center and encourage children to read it on their own or in small groups. They can read along with the audiocassette of *Pizza Party!* and write about it in their Journals.

## ✓ Comprehension Check

**ACT IT OUT**

Offer children the opportunity to act out *Pizza Party!* Provide children with props such as spoons, plastic knives, bowls, and measuring cups.

# CENTER WORKSHOPS

## Draw It!

Create a pizza on paper. Let children work in pairs to cut out a large white circle to represent the pizza dough. Then add other construction-paper cutouts on top to stand for ingredients such as red sauce, mozzarella cheese, and vegetable slices. Let children write about their pizza and/or label the different parts.

Encourage children who worked with partners to talk about their pizza-making experience.

*Observation:* Notice what kinds of shapes children cut out to make the pizza toppings.

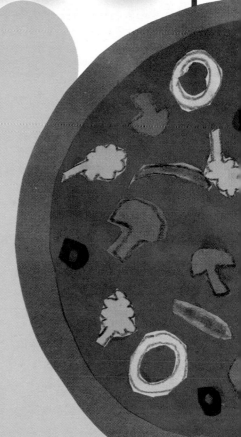

### MATERIALS

- **Construction paper**
- **Scissors**
- **Markers**
- **Glue**
- **Crayons**
- *Pizza Party!*

## Play-Dough Delight

Write "We Make Play Dough!" on chart paper. Make the play dough, using the recipe.

As children perform each step, ask them what they are doing. Write what they say on a large chart, following the format of *Pizza Party!* For example: "We add flour. We mix."

When the dough is ready, encourage children to play with it. Ask children how they are using the play dough, and add their comments to the chart.

Finally, read the chart with children. Discuss how they worked together.

*Observation:* Notice how children describe what they're doing. Do they say "we" or "I"?

### MATERIALS

- **Flour**
- **Salt**
- **Utensils**
- **Mixing bowl**

### Play Dough Recipe

**Ingredients:**
4 cups flour
1 ¾ cups warm water
1 cup salt
Bowl

**What To Do:**
1. Mix all ingredients together.
2. Knead 10 minutes.
3. Model as with any clay.
4. Bake at 300°F until hard or air dry a few days.

## DAY 3 OBJECTIVES

**CHILDREN WILL:**

- listen for alliteration
- recognize consonant /k/k
- write letter /k/k
- reread *Pizza Party!*
- read the High-Frequency Reader: *We Are Painting*
- match written to spoken words
- identify the high-frequency words: *we, are*
- engage in Center Workshops

## MATERIALS

- *Pizza Party!*
- High-Frequency Reader: *We Are Painting*
- My Read and Write Book, p. 24
- My Alphabet Book, p. 13

The Big Book is available on audiocassette in the Literacy Place Listening Center.

My Alphabet Book, p. 13

# Revisit the Big Book

**DAILY PHONICS** *and Read the High-Frequency Reader*

## Consonant /K/k

### Ⓐ PHONOLOGICAL AWARENESS

**Alliteration** Write the following alliterative sentence on the chalkboard:

**Kevin keeps ketchup in the kitchen.**

Read aloud the sentence, and have children repeat it. Then ask children to gently kick one foot each time they hear **/k/.**

### Ⓑ CONNECT SOUND-SPELLING

**Introduce Consonant /k/k** Page through *Eating the Alphabet* until you get to the *Kk* page. Point out to children that the letter *k* stands for /k/ as in **kiwifruit.**

- Ask children to say the sound with you.
- Have children point to the *Kk* ABC card and name the picture.

## Letter Formation

**WRITE THE LETTER**

Write *Kk* on the chalkboard. Point out the capital and small forms of the letter and model how to write the letter using the rhyme provided.

- Have children write both forms of the letter in the air with their fingers. Ask children to make the letter's sound as they practice writing.

### Kk

Look at a **K** and you will see,
a tall straight stick.
*(Pull down straight.)*
Add a sideways V.
*(Pull down on a slant to the center of the straight line. From the new slant, pull down on a slant to the baseline.)*

## Reread the Big Book

**Echo Read** Read *Pizza Party!* with children. Invite them to read each page right after you. Point to each word as they say it aloud. Encourage them to note high-frequency words: *to, the,* and *a.*

**Focus on Sequence** Talk about the process that the people in the story go through as they make pizza.

▶ **What would happen if the children skipped a few of the steps?**

▶ **Are there any items that the children do not need to make their pizza?**

Invite each child to draw one step in the process of making pizza. When they are done, have children hold up their pictures and arrange themselves in front of the class to show the correct order or sequence.

**READ AND WRITE INDEPENDENTLY**
**Journal** Place copies of *Pizza Party!* in the Reading Center for children to read. Children can write in their Journals about times they have helped to cook.

**Pizza Party!**

## Concepts of Print

**MATCH SPOKEN TO WRITTEN WORDS**
Display the sentence strips for *Pizza Party!*

• Ask children which word appears in each sentence *(we).* Have volunteers find each *we.*

• Remind children that many of the words in this book rhyme. Explain that rhyming words often end with the same letters.

• Invite volunteers to identify rhyming pairs by looking for words that end in the same letters. Together, say the words aloud and decide if they rhyme.

**MODIFY Instruction**

### ESL/ELD

▲ Some English language learners may have interesting stories about cooking foods from their family's country of origin. Encourage them to share some of these stories with their classmates. Support children's descriptions by asking them questions and by repeating and developing what they say. **(REAL-LIFE CONNECTIONS)**

**We Are Painting**

**My Read and Write Book,
p. 24**

# Read High-Frequency Reader

**INTRODUCE THE BOOK**

Show the book *We Are Painting* and read the title and author's name. Then ask children:

▶ **What are the children on the cover doing? What do you think the book will be about?**

▶ **What kinds of paintings do you like to do?**

**HIGH-FREQUENCY WORDS:** *we, are*

- Write the sentence stem *We are painting* _____ on the board. Read it aloud. Underline the word *We.* Then write the word *we* on a note card. Read it aloud.

- Display the card and have children read the word.

- Help children spell it aloud, clapping on each letter.

- Ask children to write *we* in the air as they state aloud each letter.

Invite children to complete the sentence stem by naming something that they would enjoy painting a picture of. Write each new sentence on the board.

Add the cards for *we* and *are* to the Word Wall.

**SHARE THE HIGH-FREQUENCY READER**

Read the story aloud. Track the print, emphasizing the concept of a word.

- Each time a color is mentioned, have children identify the color. Point to the word that names the color.

- Each time a number is given, have the children point to and count the items mentioned.

- The story also reviews consonants **/g/g** and **/h/h.** Help children use their knowledge of these sound-spellings to decode words.

**SHARED WRITING**

Invite children to work together to make a class book called *We Are Painting*.

- Help children write and complete the sentence *We are painting* _____ on a piece of paper. Have them illustrate their sentences. Bind the pages into a book and share it with the class.

# CENTER WORKSHOPS

## Tell a Story

Guide children to form small groups. Provide several different story starters such as "My favorite time to eat pizza is . . ." or "The best kind of pizza has . . ." or for the very imaginative, "Once there was an enormous pizza that was so big it . . ." Children can share, draw, and write about their ideas.

You might also place copies of *Pizza Party!* in the Art Center so children can draw pictures based on the book or on experiences triggered by it.

*Observation:* Notice what ideas children share and how they express them.

### MATERIALS

- Paper
- Markers
- Crayons
- Copies of *Pizza Party!*

## Our Own Pizza Party!

After you read *Pizza Party!* together, have your own pizza party. Write the recipe with rebus drawings on a chart, so children can create mouth-watering pizza for the whole class. Divide the group into stirrers, kneaders, spreaders, graters, and cleaners.

Follow the experience by putting out paper and crayons for children to use in drawing and writing about their cooking experiences. Send extra copies of the recipe home, so children can share it with their families.

*Observation:* How do children respond to the rebuses in the recipe?

### MATERIALS

- Rectangular baking pan
- Yeast
- Flour
- Water
- Tomato sauce
- Mozzarella
- Cheese grater

### Pizza Recipe

Put 1 cup of lukewarm water and 1 package of yeast in a mixing bowl.

Let stand 5 minutes. Stir.

Add 1 teaspoon sugar, 1 teaspoon salt, 1 teaspoon shortening.

Beat well.

Add 1 ½ cups flour.
Knead until smooth.

Divide the dough into thirds and form into balls.

Flatten, then pull and stretch gently to fit a 9 inch pan.

Let rise for 15 minutes.
Brush with olive oil.

Sprinkle with grated cheese.

Cover with tomato slices, slivers of mozzarella and oregano.

Bake 25 minutes at 425°F.

### DAY 4 OBJECTIVES

**CHILDREN WILL:**

- orally blend onset and rime
- review consonant /k/*k*
- read and respond to *Blueberries for Sal*
- recognize patterns
- read with expression
- understand story sequence
- write sentences
- engage in Center Workshops

### MATERIALS

- *Blueberries for Sal*

# Share the Read Aloud

### DAILY PHONICS

# Consonant /K/k

**A PHONOLOGICAL AWARENESS**

**Oral Blending** Say the following word parts, and ask children to put the sounds together to say the whole word.

/k/. . . eep   /k/ . . . ite   /k/ . . . iss

/k/ . . . it    /k/ . . . ing   /k/ . . . ick

**B CONNECT SOUND-SPELLING**

**The Kite's Tail** Draw a kite with a long line for a tail. Write *kite* and circle the letter *k.* Remind children that the letter *k* stands for **/k/.** Invite children to suggest words that begin with **/k/.** Write each word on the kite's tail. Have volunteers circle the letter *k.* If children suggest words that begin with *c,* explain that the sound is the same but the letter is different.

## Build Background

**ORAL LANGUAGE: BLUEBERRIES**

Bring in fresh or frozen blueberries or pictures of them. Talk about the berries with children.

► **Have you ever picked blueberries? Are they really blue?**

► **Have you eaten blueberry jam, pancakes, or muffins?**

If you have fresh or frozen blueberries, distribute a few to each child to taste. Ask children to describe the taste.

**PREVIEW AND PREDICT**

Read the title and the author/illustrator's name. Point out the Caldecott Medal for excellence in illustration.

► **Who is the girl on the cover? What is she holding?**

► **What do you think will happen in this book?**

## Share the Read Aloud

**READ WITH EXPRESSION**

Read *Blueberries for Sal* with expression, emphasizing the sounds of the blueberries being dropped into the tin pail and the characters' dialogue. Although it is a long book, the patterns in the story will keep children interested and involved.

While you read, encourage children to chime in as the sounds of the blueberries being dropped into the tin pail are repeated; "kuplink, kuplank, kuplunk."

**Blueberries for Sal**

## Respond to the Literature

**TALK ABOUT IT**

**Share Personal Responses** Listen to children's questions and wonderings about the story.

▶ **What did you think was going to happen when you saw Little Sal and her mother walking off to pick blueberries with their pails? Were your predictions right? Did you think they would meet bears?**

▶ **What did you notice about the human and animal characters? How were they the same or different?**

**THINK ABOUT IT**

**Looking for Patterns** Guide children in tying the story to the unit concept of Teamwork.

▶ **How did Little Sal and her mother and Little Bear and his mother work as a team to get work done?**

Help children understand the patterns or parallels in the story by making a comparison chart.

**MODIFY Instruction**

**GIFTED & TALENTED**

✳ Have pairs of children use the pictures in the book to retell the story. One partner can retell the pages featuring Sal. The other can retell Little Bear's story. **(WORK IN PAIRS)**

| Little Sal and Mother | Little Bear and Mother |
|---|---|
| Picked blueberries Found each other Went down Blueberry Hill | Picked blueberries Found each other Went down Blueberry Hill |

## Shared Writing

**WRITING SENTENCES**

Together with children, write sentences about blueberries on chart paper. As you share the process of writing, children can write the letters that stand for the sounds they hear in the words.

Reread what children have written. Say each sentence slowly and let children point to the words and to the period at the end of each sentence.

| Blueberries |
| --- |
| I like blueberries. |
| I like blueberry pie. |
| I like blueberry jam. |
| I like blueberry muffins. |

## Repeated Reading

**FOCUS ON SEQUENCE**

Invite children to listen for the order in which the events happen in *Blueberries for Sal*. After the rereading, discuss the sequence to help children understand the story line.

**READ AND WRITE INDEPENDENTLY**

**Journal** Place *Blueberries for Sal* in the Reading Center or the Dramatic Play Center and watch and listen to children tell one another the story as they remember its language. Children can draw and write in their Journals about their favorite characters.

## ✅ Comprehension Check

**ACT IT OUT**

Draw a large mountain on mural paper to represent Blueberry Hill. Children will enjoy adding trees, blueberry bushes, and a big rock. Place the mural on the floor or wall to use as scenery.

As you narrate the story, invite children to play the roles of Little Sal, her mother, Little Bear, his mother, and perhaps the mother crow, mother partridge, and their children. To include a larger number of children, they can also role-play the blueberry bushes, rocks, pail, and other elements in the story.

# CENTER WORKSHOPS

### Art

## MATERIALS

- **Warming tray**
- **Aluminum foil**
- **Berry-colored crayon stubs**
- **Paper**
- **Paper towels**
- **Pencils**

## Melted Crayon Art

Be especially aware of safety issues with this activity. Cover the warming tray with the aluminum foil. Under adult supervision, each child can draw on the foil with the berry-colored crayons, which will melt onto the foil.

Place a piece of paper on top of the foil, brush over it with a pencil, and remove the design.

Wipe off excess wax from the foil with a paper towel before using the tray again.

Use round, berry-shaped paper for one of the student's melted crayon pieces and mount the finished art onto a "blueberry bush" bulletin board.

*Observation:* How do children make drawings with crayons and foil?

### Cooking

## MATERIALS

(serves 5 children]
- **2 cups of berries**
- **2 bananas**
- **1 cup milk**
- **1 cup plain yogurt**
- **1/2 cup sugar**
- **Blender**
- **Plastic knives**

## A "Berry" Good Smoothie!

Assist children in following the steps of this recipe:

1. Wash, peel, and chop the fruit.
2. Put all the ingredients in the blender.
3. Blend, pour, and enjoy!

Children may want to offer ideas for foods that would be good accompaniments to the smoothie and create another menu for their final project, the "Big Book of Menus."

*Observation:* How do children use cooking tools to measure the ingredients?

## DAY 5
## OBJECTIVES

**CHILDREN WILL:**

- generate rhyming words
- recognize sound-spelling relationship for /k/k
- identify the punctuation marks
- review high-frequency words: *we, are*
- read My Book: *We Dance*
- engage in Center Workshops

## MATERIALS

- *Big Book of Rhymes and Rhythms,* p. 16
- Sentence Strips for "Humpty Dumpty"
- *Eating the Alphabet*
- My Book: *We Dance*
- My Read and Write Book, p. 25
- ABC Card: Pp

**My Read and Write Book, p. 25**

For additional practice see *Scholastic Phonics K,* pp. 59–62. See also Sound and Letter book: *Kevin.*

# Sounds and Letters

DAILY PHONICS

and Read My Book

# Consonant /k/k

**Ⓐ PHONOLOGICAL AWARENESS**

**Rhyme** Read aloud the rhyme "Humpty Dumpty" from the *Big Book of Rhymes and Rhythms.* Invite children who know this popular nursery rhyme to join in.

Before reading it a second time, ask children to listen for **/k/** in the rhyme. Emphasize the **/k/** at the beginning of *king's.* Invite children to repeat the word as you exaggerate the beginning sound.

Have children notice the rhyming pattern. Encourage them to think of other words that rhyme with *fall* and *all.*

**Big Book of Rhymes and Rhythms, p. 16**

**Ⓑ CONCEPTS OF PRINT**

Place the *Big Book of Rhymes and Rhythms,* the sentence strips for "Humpty Dumpty," and a pocket chart in the Reading Center. Then do the following:

- Read the rhyme and have children listen as you pause when you come to a comma. Have them listen to the way your voice responds to the end exclamation point.
- Reread the rhyme together. Ask volunteers to place the appropriate Sentence Strip in a pocket chart as you read each line.
- Invite volunteers to frame each word in a sentence with their fingers.
- Then have children point to all the words that begin with **Kk.**

Humpty Dumpty sat on a wall,

Humpty Dumpty had a great fall.

All the king's horses

And all the king's men

Couldn't put Humpty

Together again.

### Ⓒ CONNECT SOUND-SPELLING

**Alphabetic Principle** Remind children that the letter *k* stands for **/k/** as in *king*. Point to the ABC Card, if available. Page through *Eating the Alphabet* as children chant the letters of the alphabet. Briefly review the sound that each letter stands for, stopping on the letter *Kk*.

**ABC Book** Explain to children that they are going to make a new page for their own ABC book. Have children make suggestions of words that begin with **/k/.** When the list is complete, invite children to work together to create the *Kk* page for their ABC Books.

**Kitten or Cat Collage** Attach a picture of a kitten to one piece of poster paper and a picture of a cat to another. Review that the **/k/** sound can be made by the letters *k* or *c.* Invite children to cut out pictures of words that begin with **/k/.** Attach pictures whose names begin with *k* to the kitten half and pictures whose names begin with *c* to the cat half. Label the pictures.

### Ⓓ VOCABULARY: HIGH-FREQUENCY WORDS

Write the incomplete sentence **We are** _____ on the chalkboard. Then do the following:

- Review the two high-frequency words and, if necessary, review the read-spell-write routine for each word.

- Place the word *painting* in the blank space. Invite a volunteer to read the new sentence, which is the title of the High-Frequency Reader children read.

- Invite children to pantomime other action words for the class to guess. Write each new word children suggest on the chalkboard.

### TECHNOLOGY

 Ask children to write the words *kit, kick,* and *kite* on the **WiggleWorks Plus** Magnet Board. Invite them to arrange the words to make a mini-crossword puzzle as shown.

 The rhyme in the *Big Book of Rhymes and Rhythms* is available on the **Sounds of Phonics** audiocassette.

**We Dance**

by Dan J. Shapiro
Illustrated by Mavis Smith

SCHOLASTIC

## MODIFY Instruction

### ESL/ELD

▲ English language learners might benefit from brainstorming a list of action words before discussing how the children in the book dance. Invite volunteers to act out each action. **(BRAINSTORM)**

# Read My Book

**INTRODUCE THE BOOK**
Let children know that they are going to get their own book that they can read on their own and take home.

► **What are some things that you have fun doing with other people?**

**PREVIEW AND PREDICT**
Pass out copies of *We Dance*. Have children identify the high-frequency word *we*. Read the title and the author's and illustrator's names. Ask children about the illustration on the cover.

► **What are these children doing?**

► **What do you think this book might be about?**

**READ TOGETHER**
Read the My Book with children, tracking the print as you read. Guide children to read along in their copies, and to point out all the ways the children move as they dance.

**PHONICS**
Ask children to say the word *jump* aloud.

► **What sound do you hear at the beginning of the word? What letter stands for that sound?**

Encourage children to use other sound-spellings they have learned to help decode words.

**READ AND WRITE INDEPENDENTLY**
**Journal** Have children read *We Dance* on their own or in small groups. Provide crayons and invite children to color the illustrations. Have them write in their Journals about how they dance.

**HOME/SCHOOL CONNECTION**
Children can take home their My Books to share with family members and friends. Suggest that children play their favorite music and act out the story of *We Dance*.

# CENTER WORKSHOPS

## Cooking

### Kiwi Kabobs!

Post a sign in the Cooking Center such as "Please Keep Our Kitchen Clean." Highlight the *Kk*'s in each word. Let children know that they will make Kiwi Kabobs.

Chart or assign various roles to children before they create their kabobs. Jobs will include: washing the fruit, separating it into different bowls, slicing it, and cleaning up.

Children can gather at tables to make the kabobs. Suggest that children make a pattern with the fruit and that they challenge other children to discover the pattern.

***Observation:*** How do children show that they understand the importance of teamwork in preparing the fruit and cleaning up?

### MATERIALS

- Wooden sticks
- Small plastic bowls
- Plastic knives
- Variety of fruits
- Chart paper
- Markers

## Art

### Kites of *Kk*

Children can design their own *Kk* kites by making and decorating a construction paper kite. Then they can add to the tail, words that begin with **/k/**. Encourage children to use the Word Wall and the ABC books to help them write their *Kk* words on index cards. Attach the cards to the tail of the kite and hang them in the classroom.

***Observation:*** Where do children find *Kk* words?

### MATERIALS

- Index cards
- Construction paper
- Kite patterns
- Pencils
- Crayons or markers

## DAY 6 OBJECTIVES

**CHILDREN WILL:**

- orally segment words
- recognize /l/
- read and respond to *Pizza*
- recognize sequence
- compare literature
- write a menu
- use picture clues
- engage in Center Workshops

## MATERIALS

- *Pizza*
- *Pizza Party!*
- **My Read and Write Book,** pp. 26–27

## GUIDED READING

To conclude each day's reading session, meet with guided reading groups. You might use Scholastic's Guided Reading Library or other books in your library.

## TECHNOLOGY

 Children can interact with the **WiggleWorks Plus** selection on the computer. They can also use the **WiggleWorks Plus** Tools to innovate on the selection, to complete activities in the writing area, or to develop phonics skills on the Magnet Board. For more information about **WiggleWorks Plus,** see the Technology Teaching Plan.

The song is available on the **Sounds of Phonics** audiocassette.

# Share the WiggleWorks Book

## DAILY PHONICS

## Consonant /l/

### PHONOLOGICAL AWARENESS

**Oral Segmentation: Beginning Sound** Read aloud the title "Here We Go Looby Loo." Ask children what sound they hear at the beginning of the words *Looby* and *Loo*.

- Say these words, isolating the beginning sound: *l-l-looby; l-l-loo*. Have children repeat. Then sing the song.
- During later singings, have children clap when they sing the words that begin with the sound **/l/.**

### Here We Go Looby Loo

**Here we go Looby Loo,**
**Here we go Looby Light,**
**Here we go Looby Loo,**
**All on a Saturday night.**

## Build Background

**ORAL LANGUAGE: BE A CHEF**

If possible, get a chef's hat or make one from paper. Explain that we call the hat a *chef's hat,* and that *chef* is another word for a cook. Have children try on the hat and demonstrate cooking.

**PREVIEW AND PREDICT**

Show the cover of *Pizza*. Read the title and the author's and illustrator's names. Invite children to talk about the illustrations on the cover and title page.

▶ **What is the chef holding?**

▶ **Is the pizza hot? How do you know?**

**SET A PURPOSE**

After children have previewed the illustrations, ask:

▶ **What will the book tell about pizza?**

## Read the WiggleWorks Book

**FOCUS ON SEQUENCE**

As you read *Pizza,* ask children to describe what the chef is doing in each picture.

▶ **What does this book show you how to make?**

▶ **Is there a special order to what you must do?**

Encourage children to see that the book gives the steps to making pizza, page by page, in order. Together, look at the recipe at the back of the book. Point out that you number the steps to follow in a recipe.

Pizza

## Respond to the Literature

**TALK ABOUT IT**

**Share Personal Responses** Ask children to share experiences they have had making pizza or seeing pizza being made.

▶ **What kinds of toppings go on pizza?**

▶ **What is your favorite kind of pizza?**

▶ **Do you think it would be fun to make pizza?**

**THINK ABOUT IT**

**Compare and Contrast** Display the books *Pizza Party!* and *Pizza.* Encourage children to compare and contrast the two books.

▶ **Do the people in both books make pizza the same way?**

▶ **How are the words the same? How are they different?**

Point out that *pizza* is the Italian word for *pie.*

▶ **How is a pizza like a pie?**

### MODIFY Instruction

#### ESL/ELD

▲ Children may have difficulty with some of the words from the book. Read aloud and pantomime each of the four words with initial consonant clusters starting with *s* (*stir, spread, sprinkle, smell*). Have children repeat the words while pantomiming. While you read the book, ask them to raise their hands as they hear each word. **(PANTOMIME)**

### TECHNOLOGY

Have children read the story on **WiggleWorks Plus** until they are familiar with the sequence of events. Then ask them to go to the Write area and list the order of events as they remember them. Encourage them to use the Stamp tool to illustrate.

**My Read and Write Book,
pp. 26–27**

## Shared Writing

**CREATE A
MENU**

Invite children to create a menu for a pizza parlor. Provide several menus from pizzerias and read them aloud.

Distribute construction paper and markers. Show children how to fold the paper in half so that it opens as a menu. Children can illustrate the front and then write on the inside the names of different kinds of pizza they want to serve.

### Pizza Menu

| | |
|---|---|
| White pizza | Pizza with peppers |
| Cheese pizza | Pizza with sausage |
| Pizza with pepperoni | Pizza with spinach |
| Pizza with mushrooms | Pizza with olives |

## Repeated Reading

**DECODING
STRATEGIES**

The words and pictures in *Pizza* are a perfect match. Both tell the reader the steps in making pizza. Invite children to reread the book keeping this connection in mind. If children are having problems reading the words, guide them to use the pictures and sound-spellings they have learned.

**READ AND
WRITE
INDEPENDENTLY**

**Journal** Invite children to read *Pizza* and *Pizza Party!* on their own. Suggest that children think of their own combinations of toppings for a pizza and draw or write about their special pizza creation in their Journals.

## ☑ Comprehension Check

**ACT IT OUT**

Invite children to act out the steps of making a pizza on each page of the story as you read it aloud once more. Encourage them to use facial expressions in a way that captures the enthusiasm of the chef.

# CENTER WORKSHOPS

## Equal Parts

Invite children to decorate the paper circles to look like pizzas. Let them pretend they will be sharing a pizza with different numbers of friends and that each friend should receive the same size slice of pizza.

Encourage children to cut the pizzas into equal parts to share with 2, 3, 4, or 6 people. Show children how they can fold the pizza to find out where to cut it.

Invite children to glue the pieces onto chart paper and write the number of slices. Guide children to work with friends and to talk about how they cut the slices so that they would be the same size.

*Observation:* Notice how children decide how to divide their pizzas into equal parts.

### MATERIALS

• Large paper circles
• Coloring materials
• Scissors
• Glue
• Chart paper

## Pizza Parlor

Children can create a pizza parlor with pizzeria props in the Dramatic Play Center. Encourage children to use teamwork and to decide together who will play the roles of waiter, dough twirler, pizza maker, pizza baker, cashier, and customers. Use the pizza menus children created.

*Observation:* How do children work together to make their pizza parlor run smoothly?

### MATERIALS

• Chef's hat
• Pizza menus
• Modeling clay
• Pizza tools
• Rolling pin
• Box for cash register
• Play money

## DAY 7 OBJECTIVES

**CHILDREN WILL:**

- listen for alliteration
- identify and write consonant /l/
- participate in reading a poem
- recognize rhyming words
- identify question marks
- explore numbers and colors
- engage in Center Workshops

## MATERIALS

- *Teamwork,* SourceCard 3
- *Eating the Alphabet*
- High-Frequency Reader: *We Are Painting*
- My Alphabet Book, p. 14

My Alphabet Book, p. 14

# Read the SourceCard

 DAILY PHONICS

 and Read the High-Frequency Reader

## Consonant /l/

### Ⓐ PHONOLOGICAL AWARENESS

**Alliteration** Write the following alliterative sentence on the chalkboard:

***Lovely Lucy loves licking lemon lollipops.***

Read aloud the sentence and ask children what sound they hear at the beginning of each word. Then invite children to repeat the sentence and count the number of times they hear /l/.

### Ⓑ CONNECT SOUND-SPELLING

**Introduce Consonant /l/** Page through *Eating the Alphabet* until you get to the *Ll* page. Point out that the letter *l* stands for /l/ as in *lemon*.

- Ask children to say the sound /l/ with you.
- Say the names of the fruits and vegetables in the illustration and ask children to exaggerate the sound /l/ at the beginning of each word.

## Letter Formation

**WRITE THE LETTER**

Write *Ll* on the chalkboard. Point out the capital and small forms of the letter. Model how to write each form using the rhymes provided.

- Have children write both forms of the letter in the air with their fingers. Ask children to make the letter's sound as they practice writing.

| L | l |
|---|---|
| **Lucky Lion leaps straight down,** *(Pull straight down.)* **Then takes off heading straight for town.** *(Pull straight across.)* | **Let's start at the top to make a line,** **Pull it down, so straight and fine.** *(Pull straight down.)* |

## Share the SourceCard

**SIDE ONE**

**Explore Fruits and Vegetables** Guide children to look at the photograph of fruits and vegetables. Read the question, "What fruits and vegetables do you see?"

- Encourage children to talk about the different fruits and vegetables in the picture. Talk about the different places people get fruits and vegetables.

- Talk together about the signs in the photograph. Read the question, "What do the signs say?" and encourage children to talk about the words and numbers on the signs.

**Side One**

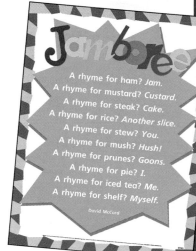

**SIDE TWO**

**Read a Poem** Read the poem on side two of the SourceCard, putting emphasis on the rhyming words at the end of each line. Remind children how words rhyme.

- Point out the common word endings of some of the rhyming pairs, such as *-am, -ice, -ush, -elf.*

- Recite the poem again, guiding children to say it along with you. Pause after each question to allow children to supply the rhyming word.

- Invite children to think of other words that rhyme with each pair.

**Side Two**

## Shared Writing

**ANSWER A QUESTION**

Show children the line "A rhyme for pie? I." and have them recite it with you.

- Write the question "Who am I?" on a chart. Read it aloud. Ask children how they know it is a question. Guide them to point out the question mark at the end.

- Children can answer the question by drawing pictures of themselves on the chart. Write *I am* _____ next to each self-portrait and have each child complete the sentence by writing his or her name.

**MODIFY Instruction**

### ESL/ELD

▲ Continue to reinforce the concept of rhyming words by encouraging children to invent their own rhymes, using real and nonsense words. This flexibility will provide security for children who are less familiar with English vocabulary. **(RHYME)**

**We Are Painting**

## ESL/ELD

▲ Encourage children to talk about pictures they have created using paint or crayons. Have them try to recall what colors they may have used. Name colors not mentioned in the book and have them repeat the color names after you. **(MAKE CONNECTIONS)**

---

# Revisit High-Frequency Reader

**REREAD THE BOOK**

Reread the book *We Are Painting* together.

Have children read the two high-frequency words in the title that they have already learned *(we, are)*. Review these words. Have children identify the word *painting*.

**DECODING STRATEGIES**

As you go through the book, point to each word, the initial letter, any other sound-spellings children have learned, and the picture clue. Pause long enough for children to read before you do. Model blending words, as needed.

**Think Aloud** *At the beginning of the word, I see the letter* h. *I know that* h *stands for* /h/. *In the picture I see horses. The word* horses *begins with* /h/. *The word* horses *makes sense in this sentence.*

**CONCEPTS OF PRINT: SENTENCES**

Show the sentence strip for page one. Point out how the sentence begins with a capital letter and ends with a period. Have a child point to the first word in the sentence and the period. Continue with others.

| We are painting green grass. |
|---|

| We are painting 5 red flowers. |
|---|

**ORAL LANGUAGE: NUMBERS AND COLORS**

Point out the numbers and color words on each page. Have children name each numeral and point to the artwork that represents each number and the artwork that goes with the color words.

**READ FOR FLUENCY**

Give each child their own copy of *We Are Painting*.

Invite children to read their books with a partner. Partners can take turns reading the pages and counting the items the children are painting.

**READ AND WRITE INDEPENDENTLY**

**Journal** Place copies of the High-Frequency Reader in the Reading Center. Children can draw or write in their Journals about a picture they would like to add to the mural in the story.

**HOME/SCHOOL CONNECTION**

Children can take home their High-Frequency Reader and work with family members on a new book about what they like to do at home.

# CENTER WORKSHOPS

**Writing**

## A Picture Rhyming Book

Children can work together to make a big book of the poem "Jamboree." Read the poem again, writing each line on a separate sheet of chart paper. As you write each line, talk about how children can illustrate the two rhyming words.

- Give each group two or three charted lines of the poem. Let children illustrate each line.

- When everyone is done, staple the pages together to make a big book. Read the poem together, exploring the illustrations the children made.

*Observation:* What illustrations do children suggest for different lines of the poem?

### MATERIALS

- Chart paper
- Markers
- Crayons
- SourceCard

**Dramatic Play**

## Our Fruit and Vegetable Stand

Let children make a pretend fruit and vegetable stand. Guide them to write labels and price tags for the fruits and vegetables they will sell.

- Children can make and find other props to represent the different fruits and vegetables, the cash register, and the other things that they want to have in their store.

- Children will enjoy taking turns being the store owners and the customers.

*Observation:* What signs do children make for their store? Do they use numbers, print, or both?

### MATERIALS

- Paper
- Markers

## DAY 8

## DAY 8 OBJECTIVES

**CHILDREN WILL:**

- orally blend word parts
- review consonant /l/
- read and respond to *Sione's Talo*
- recognize story pattern
- use picture clues
- explore problems and solutions
- engage in Center Workshops

## MATERIALS

- *Sione's Talo*
- Magnet Board

## TECHNOLOGY

Children can use the **WiggleWorks Plus** Magnet Board to create words that contain the **/l/** sound. Then invite them to create their own illustrations for gardens in the **WiggleWorks Plus** writing area. They can use the drawing tools to show what they plant and grow. For more technology activities, see the Technology Teaching Plan.

# Share the Read Aloud

## Consonant /l/

### Ⓐ PHONOLOGICAL AWARENESS

**Oral Blending** Say the following word parts aloud. Ask children to blend them. Provide feedback and modeling when necessary.

| /l/ . . . ike | /l/ . . . id | /l/ . . . og |
|---|---|---|
| /l/ . . . uck | /l/ . . . amp | /l/ . . . ast |

### Ⓑ CONNECT SOUND-SPELLING

**Leafy Words** Write the word *leaf* on the chalkboard. Say the word aloud, emphasizing the beginning **/l/** sound. Circle the letter *l* and remind children that the letter *l* stands for **/l/.** Draw a tree on chart paper. Invite children to name other words that begin with **/l/.** Write each word near the tree. Invite volunteers to come up, draw a leaf around the word, and circle the letter *l.*

## Build Background

**ORAL LANGUAGE: PLANTS**

Invite children to talk about the kinds of trees and flowers that grow in their neighborhoods. Then tell them that they will be reading about a very warm place where different kinds of plants grow. Explain that the coconut tree on page 7 grows in some very warm places. Have children point to the coconuts high in the tree. Invite children who have tasted coconut to describe its taste.

**PREVIEW AND PREDICT**

Read the title and the author's and illustrator's names. Tell children that the plant on the cover is called *talo*, and that the man's name is *Sione.* Ask children to describe what is happening in the cover illustration.

▶ **What is Sione doing?**

▶ **What do you think will happen in this story?**

## Share the Read Aloud

**RECOGNIZE STORY PATTERN**

As you read the story, help children recognize the pattern that repeats over and over again. As children recognize the pattern, encourage them to chime in. Pause after each new character is introduced and ask:

▶ **What do you think will happen next?**

Guide children to observe how the pictures show the family's way of life. Take time to explore the surroundings and the kinds of tasks the family members are doing.

**Sione's Talo**

## Respond to the Literature

**TALK ABOUT IT**

**Share Personal Responses** Ask children to tell what they found interesting.

▶ **Which picture did you like best?**

▶ **Look at page 5. What is the mother doing? What might she be making?**

▶ **Does this story remind you of another tale you have read? How is this story like *The Great Big Enormous Turnip?***

**SING A SONG**

To emphasize a sense of community members helping each other, sing "The More We Get Together" with children.

**THINK ABOUT IT**

**Discuss Story Ending** Invite children to talk about the ending of the story.

▶ **How did a tiny ant help pull the strong talo out of the ground?**

Invite children to tell in their own words how the ant caused a kind of "chain reaction."

Have children study the picture at the end of the story.

▶ **Is talo something good to eat? How do you know? How do you think the family is feeling?**

**MODIFY Instruction**

### GIFTED & TALENTED

✳ **Have children summarize the story. Ask them to share examples of other tales that are similar. Have them read stories in which a small or lowly creature does a "big" deed. (SUMMARIZE)**

## Shared Writing

**REPEATED PHRASES**

Write this sentence on chart paper and read it together:

**Sione pulled, and pulled, and pulled.**

- Have children create new episodes for the book by thinking of new characters.
- Then invite children to repeat the sentence, substituting their character's name for *Sione*.
- Write the new sentences on a chart and read them together. Invite children to illustrate their sentences.

## Repeated Reading

**TALK ABOUT SETTING**

As you reread the story, direct children's attention to the illustrations. When each new character appears, ask what he or she is doing. Explain how an illustrator makes a setting or place come to life.

- Ask children what they can tell about Sione's home from looking at the pictures.
- Have children imagine this story took place where they live. Ask how the illustrations would be different.

**READ AND WRITE INDEPENDENTLY**

**Journal** Place *Sione's Talo* in the Reading Center. Children may enjoy drawing Sione and his family working together to solve another problem. Children can create story episodes in their Journals that go along with their pictures.

## ✅ Comprehension Check

**ACT IT OUT**

Invite children to reenact the story through pantomime. Children can create props or costumes for their dramatic play, but should concentrate on using their faces and bodies to tell the story.

# CENTER WORKSHOPS

## Science

### MATERIALS

- Carrots
- Saucers

## Taking Root

Show children carrots and talk about how they are really the root of the carrot plant. Cut the top inch off a number of carrots. Give small groups of children a carrot top and a saucer, and guide them to pour water in the saucer. Place the saucers in a warm, bright place.

- Encourage children to write and draw in their Journals about the carrots. What do they think will happen?

*Observation:* Listen to the children describe what they are doing. How do they show their observations?

## Science

### MATERIALS

- Commercial ant farm
- Magnifying glasses
- Bits of fruit
- Outdoor ants

## Observe an Ant Colony

If you happen to have an ant farm in your room, allow children time to observe ant behavior. Ants live in colonies, or communities, and divide tasks among members. Some ants make tunnels; others go out in search of food, and so on.

In warm weather, it may be possible to find ants busy at work on school grounds. Fruit or other sweets will attract ants to a particular spot so children can observe them in action.

- Encourage children to answer questions such as: Do the ants work together or individually? How can ants carry food many times their weight back to their colonies?

*Observation:* Listen to how children describe what they see. What generalizations do they make?

## DAY 9 OBJECTIVES

**CHILDREN WILL:**

- review /l//l/
- connect spoken words to written words
- review the high-frequency words
- read My Book: *I Read, You Read*
- engage in Center Workshops

## MATERIALS

- *Big Book of Rhymes and Rhythms, p. 17*
- **Sentence Strips for "Mary Had a Little Lamb"**
- **Pocket chart**
- *Eating the Alphabet*
- **My Book:** *I Read, You Read*
- **My Read and Write Book, p. 28**

**My Read and Write Book, p. 28**

For additional practice see *Scholastic Phonics K,* pages 63–66. See also Sound and Letter book: *Look.*

# Sounds and Letters

 **DAILY PHONICS**

 **and Read My Book**

## Consonant /l//l/

### A PHONOLOGICAL AWARENESS

**Rhyme** Read aloud the rhyme "Mary Had a Little Lamb" from the *Big Book of Rhymes and Rhythms.* Children who are familiar with it may want to join in.

Say the words *little* and *lamb* slowly, emphasizing the beginning sound. Ask children with names beginning with /l/ to stand. Connect the sound to any other words that are visible in the classroom.

**Big Book of Rhymes and Rhythms, p. 17**

### B CONCEPTS OF PRINT

Place the *Big Book of Rhymes and Rhythms,* the Sentence Strips for "Mary Had a Little Lamb," and a pocket chart in the Reading Center. Then do the following:

- Read the rhyme together, asking children to move their arms in time with the rhythm.
- As you read each line of the rhyme again, ask a volunteer to find the Sentence Strip for that line and place it in the pocket chart.
- When the whole rhyme is assembled, invite children to point to and read the words that begin with *Ll.*
- Have children point to the words that begin with *Ll* again, frame the letter *L* or *l,* and tell whether it is an uppercase or lowercase letter.

> Mary had a little lamb,
> Its fleece was white as snow,
> And everywhere that Mary went
> The lamb was sure to go.

## ESL/ELD

▲ Develop a picture glossary of animals named in rhymes and stories to provide a visual context for children who are learning English. This strategy can help English language learners understand meanings by relating words to visual contexts. Some children may need support in identifying *Ll* in the rhyme. They may benefit from knowing how many *Ll*'s they should find in each line. **(CONTEXT CLUES)**

ⓒ **CONNECT SOUND-SPELLING**

**Alphabetic Principle** Remind children that the letter *Ll* stands for **/l/** as in *lamb*. Page through *Eating the Alphabet* as children chant the letters. Review the sound each letter stands for, stopping on the letter *Ll*. Read the words to the children and have them point to the *leek, lemon, lettuce,* and *lime*.

**ABC Book** Explain to children that they are going to make a new page for their own ABC book. Have children make suggestions of animals, objects, and people whose names begin with **/l/**. When the list is complete, children can add a special *Ll* page for their personal ABC books.

**What Is It?** Play a guessing game. Invite children to name the *l* word that answers the following clues:

▶ **When you turn this on, you can see better.** *(lamp)*

▶ **It has steps for climbing up high.** *(ladder)*

▶ **You have two of these, but only hop on one.** *(legs)*

▶ **Trees have lots of these.** *(leaves)*

Write the **/l/l** words on the board.

ⓓ **VOCABULARY: HIGH-FREQUENCY WORDS**

Write the incomplete sentence *We are* _____ on the chalkboard. Then do the following:

• Review the high-frequency words *we* and *are*. If necessary, review the read-spell-write routine for each word.

• Invite children to complete the sentence stem by naming something they are doing now such as *working, sitting, listening, looking, learning,* or *reading*. Write each new sentence on the chalkboard and invite a volunteer to read it.

## TECHNOLOGY

 Write the words *let, like,* and *look* on the **WiggleWorks Plus** Magnet Board and help children read them. Explode the words to mix up the letters. Then invite children to rewrite the words.

The rhyme in the *Big Book of Rhymes and Rhythms* is available on the **Sounds of Phonics** audiocassette.

# DAY 9

**I Read, You Read**

## Read My Book

**INTRODUCE THE BOOK**

Let children know that they are going to get their own book that they can read on their own and take home.

▶ **Do you make pictures? Do you write? Do you count things? Do we all read together?**

**PREVIEW AND PREDICT**

Distribute copies of *I Read, You Read*. Read the author's and illustrator's names. Ask children about the illustration on the cover.

▶ **What is the boy doing?**

▶ **What do you think this book might be about?**

**READ TOGETHER**

Read *I Read, You Read* with children, tracking the print as you read. Have children identify the high-frequency words *I* and *you*. Guide children to read along in their copies and to count, draw, and write in the spaces indicated.

**PHONICS**

Ask children to say the word *count* aloud.

▶ **What sound do you hear at the beginning of the word? What letter stands for that sound?**

Be sure children understand that the letters *k* and *c* sometimes stand for the same sound, as in the words *kite* and *cat*.

**READ AND WRITE INDEPENDENTLY**

**Journal** Encourage children to read *I Read, You Read* on their own or in small groups. Provide crayons and invite children to color the illustrations. Have children write about a favorite book in their Journals.

**HOME/SCHOOL CONNECTION**

 Children can take home their My Book and take turns reading with a family member or friend.

# CENTER WORKSHOPS

**Math 123**

## Lids, Lids, Lids!

Lids make a great math manipulative, and children can help you collect them from juice bottles, condiments, and other discarded jars.

Create labels that read "large lids," "medium lids," and "little lids." Children can work together to sort the lids by color or size.

If you have a large collection, children can glue them down on oaktag mats. Notice together the letter *l* in *large, little,* and *lid.*

***Observation:*** Listen to children's conversations as they work with lids. They may use other *Ll* words.

### MATERIALS

- Assorted lids
- Sorting trays and labels
- Glue (optional)

**Math 123**

## Looking at Leaves

Children can work with partners and look at the bumpy side of a leaf. One partner can cover the leaf with paint, and press paper over it to make a leaf print. The other holds the leaf steady by its stem.

When the paint dries, cut out the leaf shape.

You may want to use all of the children's leaf prints to create a large mural of a tree on the bulletin board.

Note: You can do this project without paint. Instead, rub aluminum foil over the leaf and make the print.

***Observation:*** How are the children attaching the leaves to the tree?

### MATERIALS

- Leaves (collected together or brought from home)
- Regular paint or finger paint
- Paper

# Put It All Together

## Sum It Up

**TALK ABOUT TEAMWORK**
Engage children in a conversation about cooperative activities they've participated in during the unit. What things have they been able to do better as a group than by themselves? Encourage children to talk about how teamwork can make tasks easier, can help solve problems, and can make learning more meaningful.

**ORAL LANGUAGE: SONG**
Sing the song "The More We Get Together" with children, holding hands in a large circle.

You can substitute *play*, *sing*, or other words for *get*.

### The More We Get Together

The more we get together,

together, together,

The more we get together,

the happier we'll be.

For your friends are my friends,

and my friends are your friends

The more we get together,

the happier we'll be.

## TECHNOLOGY

Children might tape record their responses to the stories they've heard. One child can interview another about the stories.

Encourage children to use the drawing and writing tools in the **WiggleWorks Plus** Write area to complete the projects and activities.

## Language Experience Chart

**COMPARE AND CONTRAST CHART**

Display the books children have read during the previous nine days. Talk together about the books, answering any questions children may have.

Make a language chart entitled "We Can Do More When We Do It Together!" Talk together about how the people or animals need one another in each of the books. Write children's responses on the language chart, which might look like the one shown below. Keep the chart on display as part of the documentation of the work children have been doing.

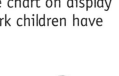

### We Can Do More When We Do It Together!

| Pizza Party! | Blueberries for Sal | Sione's Talo |
|---|---|---|
| We need one another to make pizza. | Sal and her mother need each other. Little Bear and his mother need each other. | Sione needs help from his family. The family needs help from a little ant. |

**Observation:**

How are children doing? Are they:
- working together to make a language chart?
- comparing the stories among themselves?
- using the story language from the various books?
- filling their retellings with details?

**EXTRA HELP**

Help children identify the need for someone else's help in each story as you complete the chart. Ask simple and specific questions such as:

> Who did Sal need?

> Who did Little Bear need?

> Who helped Sione and his family?

**(GUIDED QUESTIONS)**

## Assessment

After your mid-year review, use the following for children who need additional practice in any or all of the areas assessed:

### PHONOLOGICAL AWARENESS

See Scholastic's Phonemic Awareness Kit. This kit contains a 13-week intervention program.

### ALPHABET RECOGNITION

Work with children using Alphabet books and ABC Cards. Make sure your work includes recognizing letters out-of-order.

### PHONICS

Use the materials in *Scholastic Phonics K.* Continue to work with children on generating and reading words.

### HIGH-FREQUENCY WORDS

Continue to review each word using the read-spell-write approach. Work with children individually or in small groups as they reread the High-Frequency Readers.

**DAILY PHONICS**

# Mid-year Review

### A PHONOLOGICAL AWARENESS

Begin your mid-year review by assessing children's phonological awareness abilities. See the Phonological Awareness Assessment available in the Kindergarten Assessment Handbook. Use the following parts of each section.

**Part A:** Initial Sounds

**Part B:** Oral Blending

**Part C:** Syllables/Rhyming

### B ALPHABET RECOGNITION

Next focus on Alphabet Recognition. Show children the Letter Names Test in the Kindergarten Assessment Handbook. The alphabet letters on this page appear out-of-order and in either uppercase or lowercase form.

Work with individual children. Point to each letter on the page and have the child tell you the letter name.

### C PHONICS

Continue your mid-year review by focusing on the sound-spellings children have learned. On index cards, write the letters *Aa–Ll*.

Work individually with children. Show each card. Have children name the letter and say the sound it stands for. Ask them to name a word that begins with that sound.

### D HIGH-FREQUENCY WORDS

Make a chart, such as the one below, to show the high-frequency words already introduced. Work individually with each child. Point to each word. Ask the child to read it.

| | | | |
|---|---|---|---|
| 1. I | 4. to | 7. you | 10. the |
| 2. see | 5. am | 8. can | 11. we |
| 3. like | 6. a | 9. my | 12. are |

# WEEKS 5 AND 6
# PROJECT

## "Big Book of Menus"

Throughout the Teamwork unit, children have explored working together and helping each other. In the Weeks 1 and 2 project, children worked together to make a daily menu. In Weeks 3 and 4 they shared recipes from home and school, working together to explore different ways of doing things and creating a "Big Book of Recipes." For the final unit project, children will use the recipes they collected to create a "Big Book of Menus" and will host a family pot luck get-together.

Review the big book of recipes children created, and ask children to think of which foods would go together as a meal. Guide children to choose foods they like from their recipe book and organize them into meals. Write each meal children create on a separate sheet of chart paper.

### MATERIALS

- **Big Book of Recipes**
- **Chart paper**
- **Markers**
- **Crayons**
- **My Read and Write Book, pp. 29–32**

### BENCHMARKS

**Monitor children's progress. Are they**

- working together and helping one another?
- demonstrating active listening skills?
- constructing meaning from pictures and print?

- Guide children to form groups, and divide the menus among them. Invite children to illustrate each menu. Children can design and illustrate a cover with the title "Big Book of Menus." List all of the children as the authors and illustrators.

- When the book is illustrated, review it together. Leave the book unbound, so that you can add the menu for the family pot luck get-together.

### Family Get-Together

At the end of Week 4 you wrote a letter inviting the families to come to a pot luck get-together and bring a favorite dish. Now it's time to get together!

- Have a family pot luck get-together with family members and friends. You and the children can prepare some of your favorite foods to share with the families, who will bring their favorite foods.

- Display the bound "Big Book of Recipes" and the "Big Book of Menus" for family members to enjoy. Also display the charts you made in Weeks 1–6 on which you compared and contrasted the books children explored and any other creations children wish to share.

Take pictures during this celebration to add to the class portfolio and to provide documentation of children's work.

# TEACHER RESOURCES
# BIBLIOGRAPHY

## Books for Sharing

☀ Cultural Connection   ★ Kid Picks   🦋 Science   🌐 Social Studies   ▦ Math   🎭 The Arts

## WEEKS 1 AND 2

**At the Laundromat**
*by Christine Loomis
illustrated by Nancy Poydar*
Scholastic, 1994 🌐 ☀
Visit another place in the community where people help one another.

**Go and Hush the Baby**
*by Betsy Byars
illustrated by Emily McCully*
Viking, 1982 ★ 🌐 🎭
Will helps his mother by keeping the baby entertained.

**Mr. McGill Goes to Town**
*by Jim Aylesworth
illustrated by Thomas Graham*
Henry Holt, 1989 🌐 🎭
Several people end up helping Mr. McGill and one another in this cumulative, rhyming story.

**My Mama Needs Me**
*by Mildred Pitts Walter
illustrated by Pat Cummings*
Lothrop, 1983 🌐 ☀
Jason, a young African-American boy, is reassured to find that he can help with the new baby.

**On Mother's Lap**
*by Ann Herbert Scott
illustrated by Glo Coalson*
Scholastic, 1995 ☀ ▦
There's room on mother's lap for both an Inuit boy and his baby sister.

## WEEKS 3 AND 4

**Cleversticks**
*by Bernard Ashley
illustrated by Derek Brazell*
Crown, 1992 ☀ 🌐
Ling Sung and his classmates share their special skills with one another.

**Clive Eats Alligators**
*by Alison Lester*
Houghton Mifflin, 1986
🌐 ★
This fun book shows how every child in a group is special in their own way.

**Daydreamers**
*by Eloise Greenfield
illustrated by Tom Feelings*
Dial, 1981 ☀ 🎭
Poems reveal the wishes and memories of several African-American children.

**I Have a Friend**
*by Keiko Narahashi*
McElderry Books, 1987 🦋 ☀
A Japanese boy describes his closest friend, his shadow.

**A Lion for Lewis**
*by Rosemary Wells*
Dial, 1982 ★ 🌐
A lion suit helps Lewis choose what he wants to be when he plays with his older siblings.

## WEEKS 5 AND 6

**Alligator Arrived With Apples: A Potluck Alphabet Feast**
*by Crescent Dragonwagon
illustrated by José Aruego and Ariane Dewey*
Macmillan, 1987 🌐
A colorful alphabetic array of animals creates a potluck feast.

**Feast for 10**
*by Cathryn Falwell*
Scholastic, 1993 ▦ ☀
Children help their mother shop as an African-American family prepares a big dinner.

**Frannie's Fruits**
*by Leslie Kimmelman*
HarperCollins, 1989 🌐 🦋
From May to September, the whole family works together on the fruit stand.

**How the Guinea Fowl Got Her Spots**
*retold and illustrated by Barbara Knutson*
Carolrhoda, 1990 ☀ 🎭
The Guinea Fowl and the Cow protect each other in this East African folk tale.

**Machines at Work**
*by Byron Barton*
HarperCollins, 1987 🌐 🦋
Men and women work together on roads and buildings.

## Books With Phonic Elements

**Go, Dog, Go!**
*by Phil D. Eastman*
Random House, 1961
Many kinds of dogs busy themselves with different activities. (G)

**Happy Hiding Hippos**
*by Bobette McCarthy*
Bradbury Press, 1994
Happy hippos hide all over town in this bouncy rhyming story. (H)

**Inch by Inch**
*by Leo Lionni*
Scholastic, 1994
This classic story introduces an inchworm who can measure anything. (I)

**Kisses**
*by Alice McLerran
illustrated by Mary Morgan*
Scholastic, 1993
A rhyming text cozily talks about kids and kisses. (K)

**Lambs for Dinner**
*by Betsy and Giulio Maestro*
Crown, 1978
Mr. Wolf wants to have the lambs for dinner. Should they let him in? (L)

**Norma Jean, Jumping Bean**
*by Joanna Cole
illustrated by Lynn Munsinger*
Norma Jean, a kangaroo, naturally likes to jump. (J)

# Books in Other Languages

## Spanish

**El Leon de Luis**
*by Rosemary Wells*
Lectorum, 1988
A lion suit helps Lewis choose what he wants to be when he plays with his older siblings.

**El día de Miranda para bailar**
*by Jackie Jasina Schaefer*
Libros Colibrí, 1994
Miranda does a dance to thank the animals for the fruit they bring her.

## Chinese

**Peter's Chair**
*by Ezra Jack Keats*
Shen's Books and Supplies
In this Chinese translation Peter learns to accept his new baby sister.

## Korean

**Mii-Chan's First Errand**
*by Yoriko Tsutsui*
Multicultural Distributing Center
Mii-Chan is proud to help by setting off to run an errand.

# Author Study: Robert McCloskey

**Make Way for Ducklings**
Viking, 1941
In this Caldecott Medal-winning book, baby ducks and their mother make their way safely from the Charles River to the Public Gardens.

**One Morning in Maine**
Viking, 1952
Set along the Maine seacoast, this is the story of a young girl who loses her tooth before making a wish.

**Time of Wonder**
Viking, 1957
Readers experience the seasonal changes from spring and summer into fall as they read about everyday experiences on an island off the coast of Maine.

**Lentil**
Viking, 1940
In this picture book, a young boy cannot sing but learns to play the harmonica.

# Teacher's Bookshelf

**Ezra Jack Keats: Artist and Picture-Book Maker**
*by Brian Alderson*
Pelican, 1994
This book features beautiful reproductions of Keats's art and a solid account of his life.

**Winnie-the-Pooh on Management**
*by Roger E. Allen*
Dutton, 1994
A favorite bear and his friends explain basic management principles.

**You Can't Say You Can't Play**
*by Vivian Gussin Paley*
Harvard University Press, 1992
A kindergarten teacher introduces a new rule and writes about its effects in her classroom.

# Technology

*For more information about Scholastic's technology, call 1-800-SCHOLASTIC*

## Software

**WiggleWorks Plus**
Scholastic (Win/Mac)
This CD-ROM component for Kindergarten through Grade 2 of Literacy Place supports children's language development. Its activities integrate reading, writing, listening, and speaking.

**I Spy**
Scholastic (Win/Mac)
These scavenger-hunt games build reading, math, problem-solving, and logic skills.

**Scholastic Reading Counts!**
(Formerly "The Electronic Bookshelf") This reading motivation/management program is for students at all reading levels.

**Usborne's Animated First Thousand Words**
Usborne/Scholastic (Win/Mac)
This vocabulary tool introduces pre- and beginning readers to English and Spanish words.

**Huggly's Sleepover: I'm Ready for Kindergarten**
Scholastic (Win/Mac)
The first software with a complete balance of essential skills for Kindergarten.

## Internet

**www.scholasticnetwork.com**
This comprehensive online curriculum service for grades K-8 features unit-by-unit extensions for Literacy Place.

**www.scholastic.com**
Scholastic's corporate web site includes Literacy Place resources and unit-related Internet links.

**Other Sites**
The Internet is growing and changing every day, so be sure to preview all sites before your students visit them.

# Scope and Sequence

| | GRADE | K | 1 | 2 | 3 | 4 | 5 |
|---|---|---|---|---|---|---|---|
| **READING** | | | | | | | |
| **Print Awareness** | | | | | | | |
| recognize that print messages represent spoken language and convcys meaning | | ● | ● | | | | |
| knows print moves left-right, top-bottom | | ● | ● | | | | |
| understands that written words are separated by spaces | | ● | ● | | | | |
| know the difference between individual letters and words | | ● | ● | | | | |
| know the difference between capital and lower-case letters | | ● | ● | | | | |
| know the order of the alphabet | | ● | ● | | | | |
| recognize conventions of capitalization and punctuation | | ● | ● | | | | |
| understand that spoken words are represented in written language by specific sequences of letters | | ● | ● | | | | |
| recognize parts of a book | | ● | ● | ● | ● | ● | ● |
| recognize that there are correct spellings | | ● | ● | ● | ● | ● | ● |
| recognize distinguishing features of paragraphs | | | | ● | ● | ● | ● |
| **Phonological Awareness** | | | | | | | |
| divide sentences into individual words | | ● | ● | ● | | | |
| identify, segment, and combine syllables | | ● | ● | ● | ● | | |
| produce and distinguish rhyming words from non-rhyming | | ● | ● | ● | ● | | |
| identify and isolate initial and final sounds | | ● | ● | ● | ● | | |
| blend sounds | | ● | ● | ● | ● | | |
| segment one-syllable words into individual phonemes clearly producing beginning, medial, and final sounds | | ● | ● | ● | ● | | |
| **Letter-Sound Relationships** | | | | | | | |
| name and identify each letter of the alphabet | | ● | ● | | | | |
| understand that written words are composed of letters that represent sounds | | ● | ● | | | | |
| learn and apply letter-sound correspondences of: | | | | | | | |
|     consonants (beginning, middle, end) | | ● | ● | ● | | | |
|     short vowel sounds | | ● | ● | ● | | | |
|     phonograms/word families/patterns | | ● | ● | ● | | | |
|     digraphs | | | ● | ● | ● | ● | ● |
|     blends | | | ● | ● | ● | ● | ● |
|     long vowel sounds | | | ● | ● | ● | ● | ● |
|     diphthongs | | | ● | ● | ● | ● | ● |
|     variant vowels | | | ● | ● | ● | ● | ● |
| blend initial letter-sounds with common vowel spelling patterns to read words | | ● | ● | ● | ● | | |
| decode by using all letter-sound correspondences within regularly spelled words | | ● | ● | ● | ● | ● | ● |
| use letter-sound knowledge to read decodable texts | | ● | ● | ● | ● | | |

● = direct instruction         ▨ = mastery

| Grade | K | 1 | 2 | 3 | 4 | 5 |
|---|:---:|:---:|:---:|:---:|:---:|:---:|
| **Word Identification** | | | | | | |
| decode by using all letter-sound correspondences within a word | ● | ● | ● | ● | ● | ● |
| use common spelling patterns to read words | ● | ● | ● | ● | ● | ● |
| use structural cues to recognize compounds, base words, and inflectional endings | | ● | ● | ● | ● | ● |
| use structural cues to recognize prefixes and suffixes | | | ● | ● | ● | ● |
| use root words and other structural cues to recognize derivational endings | | | ● | ● | ● | ● |
| identify multisyllabic words by using common syllable patterns | | | ● | ● | ● | ● |
| recognize high-frequency irregular words | ● | ● | ● | ● | ● | ● |
| use knowledge or syntax and context to support word identification and confirm meaning | ● | ● | ● | ● | ● | ● |
| read regular and irregular words automatically | | ● | ● | ● | ● | ● |
| locate meanings, pronunciations, and derivations of unfamiliar words using dictionaries, glossaries, and other sources | | ● | ● | ● | ● | ● |
| **Fluency** | | | | | | |
| read regularly in independent-level materials | | ● | ● | ● | ● | ● |
| read regularly in instructional-level materials | | ● | ● | ● | ● | ● |
| read orally from familiar texts | | ● | ● | ● | ● | ● |
| self-select independent-level materials | | ● | ● | ● | ● | ● |
| read silently for increasing amounts of time | | ● | ● | ● | ● | ● |
| demonstrate characteristics of fluent and effective reading | | ● | ● | ● | ● | ● |
| adjust reading rate based on purpose | | ● | ● | ● | ● | ● |
| read aloud | | ● | ● | ● | ● | ● |
| **Text Structures/Literary Concepts** | | | | | | |
| distinguish different forms of texts | ● | ● | ● | ● | ● | ● |
| understand simple story structure | ● | ● | ● | ● | ● | ● |
| distinguish fiction from nonfiction | ● | ● | ● | ● | ● | ● |
| distinguish fact from fantasy | ● | ● | ● | ● | ● | ● |
| distinguish among types of text | ● | ● | ● | ● | ● | ● |
| distinguish between roles of the author and illustrator | ● | ● | ● | ● | ● | ● |
| identify text as narrative or expository | | | ● | ● | ● | ● |
| compare communication in different forms | ● | ● | ● | ● | ● | ● |
| understand and identify literary terms | ● | ● | ● | ● | ● | ● |
| analyze characters | ● | ● | ● | ● | ● | ● |
| identify importance of setting | ● | ● | ● | ● | ● | ● |
| recognize and analyze story problem/plot and resolution | ● | ● | ● | ● | ● | ● |
| judge internal consistency or logic of stories and texts | | ● | | ● | | ● |
| recognize that authors organize information in specific ways | | ● | ● | ● | ● | ● |

# Scope and Sequence

| Grade | K | 1 | 2 | 3 | 4 | 5 |
|---|---|---|---|---|---|---|
| identify purposes of different types of texts | ● | ● | ● | ● | ● | ● |
| recognize the distinguishing features of genres | | ● | ● | ● | ● | ● |
| describe the author's perspective or point of view | | | ● | ● | ● | ● |
| **Variety of Texts** | | | | | | |
| read fiction, nonfiction, and poetry for pleasure and information | ● | ● | ● | ● | ● | ● |
| use graphs, charts, signs, captions and other informational texts to acquire information | ● | ● | ● | ● | ● | ● |
| read classic and contemporary works | ● | ● | ● | ● | ● | ● |
| read from print a variety of genres for pleasure and information | ● | ● | ● | ● | ● | ● |
| read from electronic sources a variety of genres for pleasure and information | ● | ● | ● | ● | ● | ● |
| read to accomplish various purposes | | ● | ● | ● | ● | ● |
| select varied sources, i.e., nonfiction, novels, textbooks, newspapers and magazines for information and pleasure | | ● | ● | ● | ● | ● |
| read for varied purposes, i.e., to be informed, entertained, appreciate writer's craft, and discover models for writing | | ● | ● | ● | ● | ● |
| **Vocabulary Development** | | | | | | |
| discuss meanings and develop vocabulary through meaningful/concrete experiences | ● | ● | ● | ● | ● | ● |
| develop vocabulary by listening and discussing selections read aloud | ● | ● | ● | ● | ● | ● |
| identify words that name persons, places or things, and actions | ● | ● | ● | ● | ● | ● |
| use dictionaries, glossaries, technology, and context to build word meanings and confirm pronunciation | | ● | ● | ● | ● | ● |
| demonstrate knowledge of synonyms, antonyms and multiple-meaning words | | ● | ● | ● | ● | ● |
| draw on experiences to bring meanings to words in context | | ● | ● | ● | ● | ● |
| use thesaurus, synonym finder, dictionary and software to clarify meanings and usage | | | | ● | ● | ● |
| determining meanings of derivatives by applying knowledge of root words and affixes | | | ● | ● | ● | ● |
| use curricular content areas and current events to study words | | | ● | ● | ● | ● |
| **Comprehension** | | | | | | |
| use prior knowledge and experiences | ● | ● | ● | ● | ● | ● |
| establish purposes for reading | ● | ● | ● | ● | ● | ● |
| retell or act out the order of events in stories | ● | ● | ● | ● | ● | ● |
| monitor own comprehension | | ● | ● | ● | ● | ● |
| draw, discuss, and describe visual and mental images | | ● | ● | ● | ● | ● |
| make and explain inferences, i.e., determining important ideas, causes and effects, making predictions, and drawing conclusions | | ● | ● | ● | ● | ● |
| identify similarities and differences in topics, characters, problems, and themes | ● | ● | ● | ● | ● | ● |
| produce summaries of text selections | | ● | ● | ● | ● | ● |
| represent text information through story maps, graphs, charts, outline, time line, or graphic organizer | ● | ● | ● | ● | ● | ● |

● = direct instruction          = mastery

| Grade | K | 1 | 2 | 3 | 4 | 5 |
|---|---|---|---|---|---|---|
| distinguish fact from opinion | | | ● | ● | ● | ● |
| practice different kinds of questions and tasks, including test-like questions | | ● | ● | ● | ● | ● |
| use cause and effect, or chronology to locate and recall information | | ● | ● | ● | ● | ● |
| determine main idea and supporting details | ● | ● | ● | ● | ● | ● |
| paraphrase and summarize text | ● | ● | ● | ● | ● | ● |
| draw inferences and support with text evidence and experience | | ● | ● | ● | ● | ● |
| find similarities and differences across texts in treatment, scope, organization | | | ● | ● | ● | ● |
| answer different types and levels of questions, i.e., open-ended, literal, and interpretative; multiple-choice, true-false, and short-answer | ● | ● | ● | ● | ● | ● |
| **Literary Response** | | | | | | |
| listen to stories read aloud | ● | ● | ● | ● | ● | ● |
| participate actively during a read aloud of predictable and patterned selections | ● | ● | ● | ● | | |
| respond through talk, movement, music, art, drama, and writing | ● | ● | ● | ● | ● | ● |
| describe how illustrations contribute to text | ● | ● | ● | ● | ● | ● |
| connect, compare, and contrast ideas, themes, and issues across texts | ● | ● | ● | ● | ● | ● |
| demonstrate understanding of informational texts through writing, illustrating, demonstrations | ● | ● | ● | ● | ● | ● |
| support interpretations or conclusions with examples from text | | ● | ● | ● | ● | ● |
| offer observations, make connections, react, speculate, interpret, and raise questions in response to text | ● | ● | ● | ● | ● | ● |
| interpret texts through journal writing, discussion, enactment, and media | ● | ● | ● | ● | ● | ● |
| support responses by referring to relevant aspects of the text and own experiences | ● | ● | ● | ● | ● | ● |
| **Inquiry/Research** | | | | | | |
| identify and form relevant questions for research | ● | ● | ● | ● | ● | ● |
| use pictures, print, and people to gather and answer questions | ● | ● | ● | ● | ● | ● |
| draw conclusions from information gathered | ● | ● | ● | ● | ● | ● |
| locate and use important areas of the library/media center | ● | ● | ● | ● | ● | ● |
| use alphabetical order to locate information | | ● | ● | ● | ● | ● |
| recognize and use parts of a book to locate information | ● | ● | ● | ● | ● | ● |
| use multiple sources to locate information that addresses questions | | | ● | ● | ● | ● |
| interpret and use graphic sources of information, i.e., charts, graphs, and diagrams | ● | ● | ● | ● | ● | ● |
| demonstrate learning through productions and displays | ● | ● | ● | ● | ● | ● |
| organize information in systematic ways | | ● | ● | ● | ● | ● |
| use compiled information and knowledge to raise additional unanswered questions | | | | ● | ● | ● |
| use text organizers to locate and organize information | | | ● | ● | ● | ● |
| summarize and organize information from multiple sources by taking notes, outlining ideas, or making charts | | | | ● | ● | ● |

| GRADE | K | 1 | 2 | 3 | 4 | 5 |
|---|---|---|---|---|---|---|
| **Culture** | | | | | | |
| connect own experiences with life experiences, language, customs, and cultures of others | ● | ● | ● | ● | ● | ● |
| compare experiences of characters across cultures | ● | ● | ● | ● | ● | ● |
| compare text events with own and other readers' experiences | ● | ● | ● | ● | ● | ● |
| determine distinctive and common characteristics of cultures through wide reading | ● | ● | ● | ● | ● | ● |
| articulate and discuss themes and connections that cross cultures | ● | ● | ● | ● | ● | ● |
| **LISTENING/SPEAKING** | | | | | | |
| determine purposes | ● | ● | ● | ● | ● | ● |
| respond to directions and questions | ● | ● | ● | ● | ● | ● |
| participate in rhymes, songs, conversations and discussions | ● | ● | ● | ● | ● | ● |
| listen critically to interpret and evaluate | ● | ● | ● | ● | ● | ● |
| listen to stories and other texts read aloud | ● | ● | ● | ● | ● | ● |
| identify musical elements of literary language | ● | ● | ● | ● | ● | ● |
| connect experiences and ideas with those of others | ● | ● | ● | ● | ● | ● |
| compare language and oral traditions that reflect customs, regions, and cultures | ● | ● | ● | ● | ● | ● |
| choose appropriate language for audience, purpose, and occasion | ● | ● | ● | ● | ● | ● |
| use verbal and nonverbal communication when making announcements, directions, introductions | ● | ● | ● | ● | ● | ● |
| ask and answer relevant questions, and contribute | ● | ● | ● | ● | ● | ● |
| present dramatics | ● | ● | ● | ● | ● | ● |
| gain control of grammar | ● | ● | ● | ● | ● | ● |
| learn vocabulary of school | ● | ● | ● | ● | | |
| use vocabulary to describe ideas, feelings, and experiences | ● | ● | ● | ● | ● | ● |
| support spoken language using props | ● | ● | ● | ● | ● | ● |
| retell by summarizing or clarifying | ● | ● | ● | ● | ● | ● |
| eliminate barriers to effective listening | ● | ● | ● | ● | ● | ● |
| understand major ideas and supporting evidence | ● | ● | ● | ● | ● | ● |
| interpret messages, purposes, and perspectives | ● | ● | ● | ● | ● | ● |
| identify and analyze persuasive techniques | | | ● | ● | ● | ● |
| distinguish between opinion and fact | | | | ● | ● | ● |
| monitor own understanding | | ● | ● | ● | ● | ● |
| listen to proficient models of oral reading | ● | ● | ● | ● | ● | ● |
| describe how language of literature affects listener | ● | ● | ● | ● | ● | ● |
| assess language choice and delivery | | | | ● | ● | ● |
| identify how regional labels/sayings reflect regions and cultures | | | | ● | ● | ● |
| demonstrate skills that reflect interviewing, reporting, requesting and providing information | | ● | ● | ● | ● | ● |

● = direct instruction          ▒ = mastery

| Grade | K | 1 | 2 | 3 | 4 | 5 |
|---|---|---|---|---|---|---|
| use effective rate, volume, pitch, tone | ● | ● | ● | ● | ● | ● |
| give precise directions and instructions in games and tasks | ● | ● | ● | ● | ● | ● |
| clarify and support with evidence, elaborations and examples | | ● | ● | ● | ● | ● |

## WRITING

### Penmanship/Capitalization/Punctuation

| | K | 1 | 2 | 3 | 4 | 5 |
|---|---|---|---|---|---|---|
| write own name and other important words | ● | ● | | | | |
| write each letter of alphabet, capital and lowercase | ● | ● | | | | |
| use phonological knowledge to map sounds to letters, in order to write messages | ● | ● | ● | ● | ● | ● |
| write messages left to right, top to bottom | ● | ● | ● | ● | | |
| gain control of pencil grip, paper position, beginning strokes, posture, letter formation, appropriate size, and spacing | ● | ● | | | | |
| use word and letter spacing and margins | | ● | ● | | | |
| use capitalization and punctuation, i.e., names, first letters in sentences, periods, question marks, exclamation marks, proper nouns, abbreviations, commas, apostrophes, quotation marks, contractions, possessives | ● | ● | ● | ● | ● | ● |
| write legibly by selecting cursive or manuscript, as appropriate | | ● | ● | ● | ● | ● |

### Spelling

| | K | 1 | 2 | 3 | 4 | 5 |
|---|---|---|---|---|---|---|
| write with proficient spelling of: CVC, CVC silent e, one syllable with blends | | ● | ● | ● | ● | ● |
| inflectional endings: plurals, verb tenses, drop final e when endings are added | | | ● | ● | ● | ● |
| single-syllable words with r-controlled vowels, final consonants | | ● | ● | ● | ● | ● |
| orthographic patterns, i.e., consonant doubling, dropping e, changing y to i | | | ● | ● | ● | ● |
| use resources to find correct spellings, synonyms, and replacements | | | ● | ● | ● | ● |
| use conventional spelling of familiar words in final drafts | | ● | ● | ● | ● | ● |
| spell multisyllabic words using regularly spelled phonogram patterns | | | ● | ● | ● | ● |
| write with more proficient spelling of contractions, compounds, and homonyms | | ● | ● | ● | ● | ● |
| open and closed syllables, consonant before -le, and syllable boundary patterns | | | ● | ● | ● | ● |
| spell words ending in -tion and -sion | | | | ● | ● | ● |
| spell accurately in final drafts | | ● | ● | ● | ● | ● |

### Composition/Process

| | K | 1 | 2 | 3 | 4 | 5 |
|---|---|---|---|---|---|---|
| dictate messages | ● | ● | ● | | | |
| write labels, notes, and captions for illustrations, possessions, charts, and centers | ● | ● | ● | ● | ● | ● |
| write to record ideas and reflections | ● | ● | ● | ● | ● | ● |
| generate ideas before writing on self-selected topics | ● | ● | ● | ● | ● | ● |
| generate ideas before writing on assigned topics | ● | ● | ● | ● | ● | ● |
| develop drafts | | ● | ● | ● | ● | ● |
| use available technology to compose text | ● | ● | ● | ● | ● | ● |
| revise selected drafts for varied purposes | | | ● | ● | ● | ● |
| revise drafts for coherence, progression, and logical support of ideas | | ● | ● | ● | ● | ● |

# Scope and Sequence

| Grade | K | 1 | 2 | 3 | 4 | 5 |
|---|---|---|---|---|---|---|
| edit for appropriate grammar, spelling, punctuation, and features of polished writings | | • | • | • | • | • |
| demonstrate understanding of language use and spelling by bringing pieces to final form and "publishing" | | • | • | • | • | • |
| proofread own writing and that of others | | • | • | • | • | • |
| select and use reference materials and resources for writing | | • | • | • | • | • |
| **Purposes** | | | | | | |
| dictate messages | • | • | • | | | |
| write labels, notes, and captions for illustrations, possessions, charts, and centers | • | • | • | • | • | • |
| write to record ideas and reflections | • | • | • | • | • | • |
| write to express, discover, record, develop, reflect, and refine ideas, and to problem solve | • | • | • | • | • | • |
| write to communicate with a variety of audiences | • | • | • | • | • | • |
| write in different forms for different purposes | • | • | • | • | • | • |
| write to influence | | | • | • | • | • |
| write to inform | • | • | • | • | • | • |
| write to entertain | • | • | • | • | • | • |
| exhibit an identifiable voice in personal narratives and stories | | | • | • | • | • |
| choose the appropriate form for own purpose for writing | | | | • | • | • |
| use literary devices, i.e., suspense, dialogue, figurative language | | | • | • | • | • |
| **Grammar/Usage/Mechanics** | | | | | | |
| use nouns and verbs in sentences | • | • | • | • | • | • |
| compose complete sentences and use appropriate punctuation | • | • | • | • | • | • |
| use singular and plural forms of regular nouns | | • | • | • | • | • |
| compose sentences with interesting elaborated subjects | | | | • | • | • |
| edit writing toward standard grammar and usage | | • | • | • | • | • |
| use correct irregular plurals | | | • | • | • | • |
| use singular and plural forms of regular nouns, and adjust verbs for agreement | | • | • | • | • | • |
| compose elaborated sentences and use appropriate punctuation | | | | • | • | • |
| use regular and irregular plurals correctly | | | • | • | • | • |
| write in complete sentences, varying the types | | | • | • | • | • |
| employ standard English usage, subject-verb agreement, pronoun referents, and parts of speech | | • | • | • | • | • |
| use adjectives and adverbs | | • | • | • | • | • |
| use prepositional phrases to elaborate written ideas | | | | • | • | • |
| use conjunctions to connect ideas | | | | • | • | • |
| use apostrophes in contractions and possessives | | • | • | • | • | • |
| use objective-case pronouns accurately | | | • | • | • | • |

• = direct instruction          = mastery

| | GRADE | K | 1 | 2 | 3 | 4 | 5 |
|---|---|---|---|---|---|---|---|
| **Evaluation** | | | | | | | |
| identify the most effective features of a piece by using student and teacher criteria | | | ● | ● | ● | ● | ● |
| respond constructively to others' writing | | ● | ● | ● | ● | ● | ● |
| determine how own writing achieves its purposes | | | ● | ● | ● | ● | ● |
| use published pieces as models | | ● | ● | ● | ● | ● | ● |
| review collection of own work to monitor growth | | | ● | ● | ● | ● | ● |
| apply criteria to evaluate writing | | | ● | ● | ● | ● | ● |
| review a collection of written works to determining its strengths and weaknesses, and to set goals | | | ● | ● | ● | ● | ● |
| **Inquiry/Research** | | | | | | | |
| record/dictate questions for investigating | | ● | ● | ● | ● | ● | ● |
| record/dictate own knowledge | | ● | ● | ● | ● | ● | ● |
| take simple notes from sources | | | ● | ● | ● | ● | ● |
| compile notes into outlines, reports, summaries | | | | ● | ● | ● | ● |
| frame questions, to direct research | | | ● | ● | ● | ● | ● |
| organize prior knowledge with graphic organizer | | ● | ● | ● | ● | ● | ● |
| take notes from various sources | | | | ● | ● | ● | ● |
| summarize and organize ideas | | | ● | ● | ● | ● | ● |
| present information in various forms | | ● | ● | ● | ● | ● | ● |
| evaluate own research and raise new questions | | | | | ● | ● | ● |
| **Connections** | | | | | | | |
| collaborate with other writers | | | ● | ● | ● | ● | ● |
| correspond with peers or others by e-mail or conventional mail | | | | | ● | ● | ● |
| **VIEWING** | | | | | | | |
| **Representing/Interpretation** | | | | | | | |
| describe illustrator's choice of style, elements, and media | | ● | ● | ● | ● | ● | ● |
| interpret events and ideas from maps, charts, graphics, video segments, and technology presentations | | ● | ● | ● | ● | ● | ● |
| **Representing/Analysis** | | | | | | | |
| interpret and evaluate visual image makers | | ● | ● | ● | ● | ● | ● |
| compare-contrast print, visual, and electronic media | | ● | ● | ● | ● | ● | ● |
| **Representing/Production** | | | | | | | |
| select, organize, and produce visuals to complement and extend meanings | | ● | ● | ● | ● | ● | ● |
| produce communications using technology | | ● | ● | ● | ● | ● | ● |

 # Index

## GRADE K

This index incorporates references to the Teacher's Edition for all six units in Grade K of Literacy Place. For your convenience, the index is divided into three sections, as listed below.

# Index

## SKILLS AND STRATEGIES

### Reading Skills and Strategies

#### Book Handling

**Handle Books Appropriately, PV:** T16, T23, T62, T78, T79, T115, T125; **CI:** T69

#### Build Alphabetic Knowledge

**Alphabetical Order, PV:** T15, T19, T76; **PS:** T14, T16

**Recite Alphabet, PV:** T14, T61, T76

**Recognize Letters** *Aa–Zz,* **PV:** T31, T47, T93, T123, T139; **PS:** T15, T31, T47, T61, T77, T93, T107, T139; **TW:** T15, T31, T61, T139, T144; **CE:** T15, T31, T47, T61, T77, T93, T107, T123, T139; **MI:** T15, T31, T61, T77, T123; **CI:** T15, T47, T61, T77, T88, T93, T107, T123, T139

**Write Letters** *Aa–Zz,* **PS:** T22, T68, T84, T108, T114, T130; **TW:** T22, T38, T61, T68, T84, T130; **CE:** T22, T38, T68, T84, T114, T130; **MI:** T22, T38, T68, T84, T114, T130; **CI:** T22, T38, T47

#### Comprehension/Thinking Strategies

**Constructing Meaning**

**Categories, PV:** T127; **PS:** T14, T15, T87, T106, T121; **TW:** T14, T16, T99, T141; **CE:** T41, T52, T111, T117; **MI:** T19, T33, T107; **CI:** T19, T23, T87

**Compare and Contrast Stories/Books/Ideas, PV:** T50–T51, T96–T97, T124, T142–T143; **PS:** T43, T50–T51, T96–T97, T115, T142–T143; **TW:** T50–T51, T96–T97, T126, T135, T142–T143; **CE:** T50–T51, T66, T96–T97, T112, T142–T143; **MI:** T50–T51, T66, T69, T89, T96–T97, T142–T143; **CI:** T39, T50–T51, T61, T66, T90, T96–T97, T142–T143

**Create and Interpret Graphic Organizers/Sources, PV:** T18, T26, T30, T36, T51, T71, T75, T86, T88, T93, T95, T97, T113, T119, T127, T131, T143; **PS:** T16, T18, T20, T37, T42, T43, T44, T51, T60, T65, T66, T80, T81, T86, T91, T97, T106, T111, T131, T132, T136, T143; **TW:** T15, T16, T20, T25, T42, T44, T61, T65, T82, T83, T89, T119, T143; **CE:** T14, T19, T28, T31, T34, T39, T51, T73, T79, T80, T83, T97, T106, T125, T128, T132, T143; **MI:** T19, T20, T33, T36, T39, T51, T69, T71, T73, T97, T107, T108, T110, T143; **CI:** T15, T19, T23, T36, T39, T44, T51, T60, T61, T81, T88, T89, T97, T137, T143

**Demonstrate Comprehension, PV:** T15, T16, T19, T20, T27, T28, T36, T43, T44, T51, T62, T65, T68, T72, T74, T82, T108, T111, T119, T120; **PS:** T15, T16, T19, T20, T27, T28, T36, T43, T44, T61, T66, T74, T81, T82, T90, T108, T112, T120, T128, T135, T136; **TW:** T15, T16, T19, T20, T27, T28, T35, T36, T43, T44, T61, T62, T65, T66, T73, T74, T82, T82, T89, T90, T127, T128, T135, T136; **CE:** T15, T16, T19, T20, T27, T28, T35, T36, T43, T44, T62, T66, T74, T82, T90, T108, T112, T120, T128, T136; **MI:** T15, T16, T19, T20, T27, T28, T36, T42, T44, T61, T62, T65, T66, T73, T74, T82, T90, T108, T112, T120, T127, T128, T131, T135, T136; **CI:** T16, T20, T28, T36, T44, T62, T66, T74, T82, T90, T108, T112, T120, T127, T128, T136

**Distinguish Reality/Fantasy, PS:** T90; **CE:** T27, T81

**Dramatize a Story (Act Out a Story), PV:** T16, T20, T36, T44, T62, T66, T74, T82, T108, T112, T120, T128, T136; **PS:** T16, T28, T36, T44, T62, T66, T74, T75, T82, T90, T99, T108, T112, T125, T128, T136, T143; **TW:** T20, T27, T33, T36, T44, T49, T62, T66, T74, T79, T82, T90, T95, T108, T112, T120, T128, T136; **CE:** T16, T17, T20, T35, T36, T37, T44, T51, T62, T66, T74, T82, T90, T108, T112, T128, T136; **MI:** T16, T20, T33, T36, T44, T61, T62, T66, T74, T82, T108, T112, T128, T129, T136; **CI:** T20, T37, T62, T74, T82, T90, T108, T112, T120, T128, T136, T145

**Explore/Focus on Picture Details, PV:** T15, T19, T23, T26, T28, T40, T43, T61, T64, T69, T72, T74, T78, T85, T88, T94, T106, T107, T108, T110, T115, T119, T120, T128; **PS:** T16, T19, T32, T34, T40, T42, T45, T48, T60, T65, T72, T88, T94, T115, T131, T135; **TW:** T18, T20, T26, T34, T39, T64, T69, T74, T94, T112, T126; **CE:** T18, T24, T26, T32, T34, T42, T48, T49, T65, T70, T81, T135; **MI:** T14, T15, T18, T23, T24, T26, T32, T34, T37, T39, T43, T60, T64, T65, T70, T73, T79, T81, T82, T88, T112, T115, T120, T126, T132, T140, T143; **CI:** T16, T23, T69, T85, T90, T108

**Investigate Cause/Effect, TW:** T135; **CE:** T69; **CI:** T134

**Make, Confirm, Revise Predictions, PV:** T14, T18, T26, T32, T34, T42, T48, T60, T64, T72, T78, T88, T89, T94, T106, T110, T118, T124, T126, T134, T140; **PS:** T14, T18, T19, T26, T32, T34, T42, T48, T60, T64, T65, T72, T78, T80, T82, T88, T94, T106, T110, T118, T124, T131, T134, T140; **TW:** T14, T18, T26, T32, T34, T42, T48, T60, T64, T72, T78, T88, T94, T126, T134, T140; **CE:** T14, T18, T26, T32, T34, T42, T48, T60, T65, T72, T78, T80, T88, T94, T106, T110, T118, T124, T134, T140; **MI:** T14, T18, T26, T28, T32, T35, T42, T48, T60, T64, T72, T78, T80, T88, T94, T106, T110, T118, T124, T126, T134, T140; **CI:** T14, T18, T26, T32, T42, T48, T60, T64, T73, T78, T88, T94, T106, T116, T119, T124, T126, T135, T140

**Recognize Main Ideas/Details, PV:** T15, T19, T27, T35, T43, T61, T65, T73, T81, T89, T107, T111, T119, T127, T135; **PS:** T15, T19, T27, T35, T43, T61, T65, T73, T81, T89, T107, T111, T119, T127, T135; **TW:** T15, T19, T27, T35, T43, T61, T65, T73, T81, T89, T107, T111, T119, T127, T135; **CE:** T15, T19, T27, T35, T43, T61, T65, T73, T81, T89, T107, T111, T119, T127, T135; **MI:** T15, T19, T20, T27, T35, T43, T61, T65, T73, T81, T89, T107, T111, T119, T127, T135; **CI:** T15, T19, T27, T35, T43, T61, T65, T73, T81, T89, T107, T111, T119, T127, T135

**Recreate Familiar Stories Through Pantomime, Puppets, Clay, and Story Theater, PV:** T19, T43, T44, T136, T137, T141; **PS:** T37, T49, T52, T73, T75, T108, T129, T135, T136, T145; **TW:** T29, T33, T40, T49, T71, T79, T82, T111, T123, T136; **CE:** T19, T25, T28, T69, T79; **MI:** T26, T29, T49, T133, T136; **CI:** T126, T128

**Respond to Literature/Extend Meaning/Share Ideas, PV:** T15, T19, T27, T35, T43, T61, T65, T73, T81, T89, T107, T111, T119, T127, T135; **PS:** T15, T19, T27, T35, T43, T61, T65, T73, T81, T89, T97, T107, T111, T119, T127, T135; **TW:** T15, T19, T27, T35, T43, T61, T65, T73, T81, T89, T97, T107, T111, T119, T127, T135; **CE:** T15, T19, T27, T35, T43, T61, T65, T73, T81, T89, T97, T127, T135; **MI:** T15, T19, T27, T35, T43, T61, T65, T73, T81, T89, T97, T127, T135; **CI:** T15, T19, T27, T35, T43, T61, T65, T73, T81, T89, T97, T127, T135

**Understand Sequence/Sequence the Story, PV:** T15, T69, T130, T131; **PS:** T27, T69, T99, T127; **TW:** T23, T28, T82, T115, T120, T127; **CE:** T82, T111, T120, T128, T136, T140; **MI:** T69, T115; **CI:** T28, T112

**Use Prior Knowledge, PV:** T14, T18, T26, T34, T42, T60, T64, T72, T81, T88, T106, T110, T126, T134; **PS:** T14, T18, T26, T34, T42, T60, T64, T72, T81, T88, T106, T110, T126, T127, T134; **TW:** T14, T18, T26, T34, T42, T60, T64, T72, T81, T88, T106, T110, T126, T134; **CE:** T14, T18, T26, T34, T42, T60, T64, T72, T80, T86, T88, T106, T110, T118, T126, T127, T132, T134; **MI:** T14, T18, T26, T34, T42, T60, T64, T72, T80, T88, T106, T110, T118, T126, T134; **CI:** T14, T18, T26, T35, T42, T60, T64, T73, T80, T106, T110, T126

## Descriptive/Entertaining Forms

**Illustrated Rhyming Story, PV:** T34–T35; **PS:** T110–T111; **MI:** T111

**Picture Riddle, PS:** T18–T20, T34–T35, T130–T131

**Poster (SourceCard), PV:** T38–T39, T84–T85, T130–T131; **PS:** T38–T39, T84–T85, T130–T131; **TW:** T38–T39, T84–T85, T130–T131; **CE:** T38–T39, T84–T85, T130–T131; **MI:** T38–T39, T84–T85, T130–T131; **CI:** T38–T39, T84–T85, T130–T131

**Explore Author's Craft, TW:** T65, T72; **CE:** T97; **CI:** T82

**Explore Illustrator's Craft, PS:** T23, T136; **TW:** T28, T67, T136; **CE:** T89, T135; **MI:** T65

## Explore Literary Elements

**Dialogue, PV:** T82, T90; **TW:** T44; **CE:** T48, T74; **MI:** T73, T74; **CI:** T20, T27, T115

**Explore Story Setting Through Illustration, PV:** T65; **TW:** T20, T136; **CE:** T115, T119; **MI:** T23; **CI:** T65, T89

**Focus on Characters, PV:** T23, T26, T27, T64, T65, T88, T89, T97, T112, T119, T120; **PS:** T28, T43, T73, T94, T96, T97, T119, T128;

**TW:** T23, T26, T28, T44, T73, T81, T89; **CE:** T35, T42, T65, T65, T73, T119, T121, T142; **MI:** T36, T43, T136; **CI:** T89, T120, T136

**Focus on Plot, PV:** T82; **PS:** T73, T89, T96, T97, T119, T127, T136, T142; **TW:** T27, T82, T90; **CE:** T43

**Identify Favorite Storybook Characters, Types of Stories, Authors, and Illustrators, PV:** T16, T17, T18, T20, T21, T27, T28, T35, T42, T43, T44, T61, T62, T85, T107, T108, T109, T110, T111, T112, T113, T117, T118, T120, T127, T128, T129, T140, T142, T143; **PS:** T15, T16, T19, T20, T35, T36, T39, T89, T108, T115, T121; **TW:** T14, T15, T16, T19, T20, T23, T43, T61, T62, T65, T89, T90, T95, T97, T99, T127, T145; **CE:** T14, T15, T16, T17, T19, T24, T26, T27, T29, T32, T42, T44, T64; **MI:** T16, T23, T25, T27, T28, T32, T42, T62, T65, T66, T67, T127, T128, T134; **CI:** T16, T25, T28, T61, T74, T90, T107, T135

## Phonological Awareness/Phonics

**Alliteration, PV:** T36, T42, T80, T126, T127; **PS:** T14, T22, T51, T62, T84, T93, T114, T126, T130; **TW:** T22, T38, T52, T68, T84, T114, T130; **CE:** T22, T30, T68, T84, T114, T130; **MI:** T22, T38, T84, T114; **CI:** T22

**Auditory Discrimination, PV:** T14, T84, T138; **PS:** T76; **TW:** T30; **MI:** T26, T68, T130; **CI:** T26, T38, T138

**Decoding Strategies, PS:** T40, T69, T86, T132; **TW:** T40, T86, T128, T132; **CE:** T23, T69, T86, T132; **MI:** T40, T69, T86, T132; **CI:** T40, T77, T86, T93, T115, T123, T132, T139

**Final Consonants, CE:** T60, T98; **MI:** T26, T52, T60, T106, T130, T144

**Initial Consonants, PV:** T14, T22, T60, T64, T77, T84, T88, T92, T93, T98, T122, T123, T139; **PS:** T15, T34, T38, T42, T46, T47, T48, T61, T76, T80, T92, T94, T106, T107, T123, T124, T130, T132, T134, T144; **TW:** T15, T22, T32, T34, T38, T46, T47, T52, T78, T93, T118, T126, T130, T134, T139, T140; **CE:** T22, T26, T31, T34, T38, T42, T47, T52, T60, T64, T76, T80, T110, T138, T144; **MI:** T14, T26, T31, T38, T42, T47, T68, T72, T77, T84; **CI:** T26, T30, T38, T68, T72, T76, T93, T110, T114, T139

**Match Sounds to Letters, PV:** T32, T48, T78, T94, T124, T140; **PS:** T32, T48, T78, T94, T124, T140; **TW:** T32, T48, T78, T94, T124, T140; **CE:** T32, T48, T78, T94, T124, T140; **MI:** T32, T48, T78, T94, T124, T140; **CI:** T32, T48, T78, T94, T124, T140

**Match Speech to Print, PV:** T60, T77, T110, T114, T125, T144; **PS:** T32, T122; **CE:** T76, T92, T115; **MI:** T76, T92, T115

**Oddity Task, PV:** T52, T130; **PS:** T38, T51, T72; **TW:** T14; **CE:** T38; **MI:** T60

**Onsets and Rimes. (see Phonograms)**

**Oral Blending, PV:** T125; **PS:** T42, T68, T88, T134; **TW:** T26, T42, T72, T88, T118, T134, T144; **CE:** T26, T42, T52, T72, T88, T118, T134; **MI:** T42, T72, T98, T118, T134; **CI:** T14, T68, T72, T76, T84, T88, T118, T130, T134

**Oral Segmentation, PV:** T46, T60, T64, T72, T76, T88, T118, T122, T125; **PS:** T18, T26, T34, T46, T110; **TW:** T18, T34, T46, T64, T92, T110, T126; **CE:** T14, T34, T60, T64, T80, T110, T144; **MI:** T18, T26, T46, T80, T88, T110; **CI:** T34, T64, T72, T88, T110, T118, T126, T134

**Phonic Blending, CI:** T68, T84, T106, T114, T118, T130, T134, T144

**Phonograms, CE:** T42, T47, T88, T93, T139; **MI:** T42, T47, T72, T77, T93, T118, T123; **CI:** T26, T31, T42, T47

## Recognize Literary Genres

**CE:** T14–T16, T60–T62, T106–T108; **MI:** T14–T16, T60–T62, T106–T108; **CI:** T14–T16, T60–T62, T106–T108

**Concept Book, PV:** T118–T120; **PS:** T64–T66, T68–T69; **TW:** T18–T20, T22–T23; **MI:** T26–T28, T64–T66, T68–T69, T72–T74; **CI:** T80–T82

**Information, PV:** T18–T20, T22–T23, T110–T112, T114–T115; **TW:** T110–T112, T127–T128; **MI:** T18–T20, T22–T24, T88–T90, T118–T120; **CI:** T18–T20, T22–T24, T26–T28

**Photo Essay, MI:** T18–T20, T22–T23, T126–T128

### Poetry

**Poetry/Song, PV:** T14, T18, T26, T30, T34, T35, T46, T50, T62, T64, T72, T76, T80, T92, T96, T110, T118, T122, T134, T138, T142; **PS:** T18, T30, T34, T35, T39, T46, T64, T76, T80, T92, T110, T118, T122, T126, T138, T142; **TW:** T18, T23, T30, T34, T46, T65, T76, T92, T110, T122, T126, T138, T142; **CE:** T18, T28, T30, T46, T50, T76, T80, T92, T122, T138, T142; **MI:** T30, T34, T46, T61, T64, T76, T80, T110, T111, T122, T126, T138, T142; **CI:** T18, T30, T34, T46, T50, T76, T80, T92, T122, T126, T138, T142

### Recognize Narrative Forms

**Cumulative Story, PS:** T80–T82; **TW:** T80–T82; **CE:** T110–T112, T114–T115

**Predictable Story, PV:** T34–T35, T42–T43, T64–T66, T68–T69; **PS:** T34–T35, T80–T82, T110–T112, T114–T115, T131, T143–T144; **CE:** T18–T20, T22–T23, T34–T36, T110–T112, T114–T115, T88–T90; **MI:** T110–T112, T114–T115, T126–T128; **CI:** T42–T44, T110–T112, T114–T115

**Circular Story, PS:** T64–T66, T68–T69; **CI:** T42–T44

## Vocabulary

**Collect Interesting Words, PV:** T24; **PS:** T30, T47, T60, T61, T77, T93, T106, T107, T123, T139; **TW:** T14, T15, T31, T47, T60, T61, T62, T77, T93, T128, T136; **CE:** T14, T15, T31, T47, T82, T93, T123, T139; **MI:** T14, T15, T16, T17, T31, T38, T47, T77, T93, T123, T139; **CI:** T31, T47

**Facial Expressions/Body Language, PV:** T111, T112, T115, T120, T128; **PS:** T74, T75, **TW:** T72, T74; **CE:** T65, T66, T85, T87; **CI:** T74, T117

**High-Frequency Words, PV:** T24, T31, T40, T47, T70, T77, T86, T93, T116, T123, T132, T139; **PS:** T24, T31, T40, T47, T70, T77, T86, T93, T116, T123, T132, T139; **TW:** T24, T31, T40, T47, T70, T77, T93, T116, T123, T132, T139, T144; **CE:** T24, T31, T40, T47, T70, T77, T86, T93, T116, T123, T130, T132, T139; **MI:** T24, T31, T40, T47, T70, T77, T86, T93, T116, T123, T132, T139; **CI:** T24, T31, T40, T47, T70, T77, T86, T93, T116, T123, T132, T139

**Make Word Categories, PV:** T46, T70, T86, T114; **PS:** T14, T15, T87, T106, T121; **TW:** T14, T99, T141; **CE:** T41, T52, T111, T117; **MI:** T19, T33, T107; **CI:** T94

**Story Vocabulary, PV:** T20, T40, T44, T61, T65, T72, T86, T107; **PS:** T42, T61, T108; **TW:** T31, T35, T37, T93, T127, T139; **CE:** T16, T31, T43, T47; **MI:** T47, T61, T77; **CI:** T69

# Writing and Language Arts Skills and Strategies

## Conventions of Language

### Mechanics

**Capitalize First Word of Sentence, PV:** T74; **PS:** T23, T123, T132; **TW:** T23, T40, T112, T132; **CE:** T132; **MI:** T28, T62, T69; **CI:** T16, T22, T23, T98, T122, T144

### Punctuation

**Exclamation Mark, PV:** T66, T74; **TW:** T122; **CE:** T28, T122; **MI:** T69, T86; **CI:** T30

**Period, PV:** T74; **PS:** T23, T69; **TW:** T122; **CE:** T120, T132; **MI:** T66, T69, T132; **CI:** T16, T40, T86, T98, T122, T131, T132, T144

**Question Mark, PV:** T74; **PS:** T20, T23, T69, T123; **TW:** T86, T122, T131; **CE:** T86; **MI:** T66, T69, T132; **CI:** T31, T40, T76, T86, T98, T122, T131, T132, T144

## Listening

### Demonstrate Active Listening Skills

**Follow Directions, PV:** T22, T38, T46, T109, T121, T137; **PS:** T50, I90; **TW:** T63, T85, T87, T93, T113, T121, T127, T145; **CE:** T125; **MI:** T39, T41, T64, T79, I99

**Listen to a Story/Poem, PV:** T14, T15, T18, T19, T26–T27, T30, T34, T35, T42–T43, T46, T50, T62, T64, T67, T72–T73, T76, T80, T81, T85, T88–T89, T92, T96, T110, T118–T119, T134–T135, T138, T142; **PS:** T18, T26–T27, T30, T34, T35, T39, T42–T43, T46, T52, T64, T72–T73, T76, T80, T88–T89, T92, T110, T118–T119, T122, T126, T134–T135, T138, T142; **TW:** T26–T27, T42–T43, T64, T72–T73, T80, T88–T89, T96, T110, T118–T119, T131, T134–T135, T138; **CE:** T26–T27, T30, T34, T42–T43, T46, T50, T72–T73, T88–T89, T118–T119, T126, T134–T135; **MI:** T26–T27, T34, T42–T43, T46, T64, T72–T73, T76, T88–T89, T96, T118–T119, T134–T135, T138, T142; **CI:** T18, T26–T27, T34, T42–T43, T50, T72–T73, T76, T80, T88–T89, T92, T118–T119, T122, T126, T134–T135, T142

### Listen to Each Other, to Others, and the Teacher

**PV:** T14, T15, T18, T19, T22, T23, T24, T26, T27, T30, T31, T34, T35, T38, T42, T43, T46, T47, T60, T61, T64, T65, T68, T69, T70, T72, T73, T74, T76, T77, T80, T81, T86, T88, T89, T92, T96, T106, T107, T110, T111, T114, T118, T119, T126, T127, T134, T135

**PS:** T14, T15, T18, T19, T22, T23, T24, T26, T27, T30, T31, T34, T35, T42, T43, T46, T47, T60, T61, T64, T65, T68, T69, T72, T73, T74, T76, T77, T80, T81, T86, T88, T89, T92, T106, T107, T110, T111, T114, T118, T119, T126, T127, T134, T135

**TW:** T14, T15, T18, T19, T22, T23, T24, T26, T27, T30, T31, T34, T35, T42, T43, T46, T47, T60, T61, T64, T65, T68, T69, T72, T73, T74, T76, T77, T80, T81, T86, T88, T89, T92, T106, T107, T110, T111, T114, T118, T119, T126, T127, T134, T135

**CE:** T14, T15, T18, T19, T22, T23, T24, T26, T27, T30, T31, T34, T35, T42, T43, T46, T47, T60, T61, T64, T65, T68, T69, T72, T73, T74, T76, T77, T80, T81, T86, T88, T89, T92, T106, T107, T110, T111, T114, T118, T119, T126, T127, T134, T135

# Index

T44, T62, T66, T70, T74, T82, T85, T90, T108, T112, T116, T120, T128, T131, T136

**Write With Symbols That Resemble Letters and Letter Shapes, PS:** T30, T47, T60, T61, T77, T93, T106, T107, T123, T139; **TW:** T14, T15, T31, T47, T60, T61, T62, T77, T93, T128, T136; **CE:** T14, T15, T31, T47, T82, T93, T123, T139; **MI:** T14, T15, T16, T17, T31, T38, T47, T77, T93, T123, T139; **CI:** T31, T47

## Speaking

**Demonstrate Speaking Skills**

Do a Commercial, **TW:** T62

**Engage in Conversation by Sharing Ideas**

**PV:** T14, T15, T18, T19, T22, T23, T24, T26, T27, T30, T31, T34, T35, T39, T41, T42, T43, T46, T47, T49, T50, T53, T60, T61, T64, T65, T68, T69, T72, T73, T74, T76, T77, T80, T81, T85, T86, T88, T89, T92, T96, T106, T107, T110, T111, T114, T118, T119, T126, T127, T134, T135

**PS:** T14, T15, T18, T19, T22, T23, T24, T26, T27, T30, T31, T34, T35, T42, T43, T46, T47, T52, T60, T61, T62, T64, T65, T66, T68, T70, T72, T73, T75, T77, T78, T80, T81, T86, T88, T89, T92, T106, T107, T110, T111, T114, T118, T119, T126, T127, T134, T135

**TW:** T14, T15, T18, T19, T22, T23, T24, T26, T27, T30, T31, T34, T35, T42, T43, T46, T47, T60, T61, T64, T65, T68, T69, T72, T73, T74, T76, T77, T80, T81, T86, T88, T89, T92, T106, T107, T110, T111, T114, T118, T119, T126, T127, T134, T135

**CE:** T14, T15, T18, T19, T22, T23, T24, T26, T27, T30, T31, T34, T35, T42, T43, T46, T47, T60, T61, T64, T65, T68, T69, T72, T73, T74, T76, T77, T80, T81, T86, T88, T89, T92, T106, T107, T110, T111, T114, T118, T119, T126, T127, T134, T135

**MI:** T14, T15, T18, T19, T22, T23, T24, T26, T27, T30, T31, T34, T35, T42, T43, T46, T47, T60, T61, T64, T65, T68, T69, T72, T73, T74, T76, T77, T80, T81, T86, T88, T89, T92, T106, T107, T110, T111, T114, T118, T119, T126, T127, T134, T135

**CI:** T14, T15, T18, T19, T22, T23, T24, T26, T27, T30, T31, T34, T35, T42, T43, T46, T47, T60, T61, T64, T65, T68, T69, T72, T73, T74, T76, T77, T80, T81, T86, T88, T89, T92, T106, T107, T110, T111, T114, T118, T119, T126, T127, T134, T135

**Give Directions, PV:** T38, T91; **TW:** T87, T99, T117

**Orally Present Poetry, PV:** T26, T34, T35, T36, T37, T46, T67, T72, T118; **PS:** T73, T76, T92, T112, T125, T126, T139; **TW:** T14, T31, T60, T136, T139; **CE:** T14, T31, T35, T36, T37; **MI:** T31, T47, T60, T106

**Participate in Choral Reading, PV:** T36, T62; **PS:** T69, T115; **TW:** T16, T35, T44; **CE:** T23, T26, T36, T62, T112; **MI:** T74, T128; **CI:** T115, T128

**Participate in Echo Reading, PV:** T35; **TW:** T115; **CE:** T19, T20, T35, T44, T64, T111; **MI:** T117; **CI:** T19, T81

**Recite a Chant, PV:** T26, T34, T35, T36, T37, T46, T67, T72, T118; **PS:** T73, T112, T132, T139; **TW:** T14, T31, T60, T123, T136, T139; **CE:** T14, T31, T35, T36, T37, T47, T95, T123; **MI:** T31, T47, T60, T106; **CI:** T31, T123

**Role Play, PV:** T20, T21, T41, T71, T82, T87; **PS:** T79; **TW:** T33, T35, T37, T74, T120, T129; **CE:** T29, T44, T82, T87, T136, T137; **MI:** T40; **CI:** T26, T63, T70, T108, T120, T137

**Share Experiences**

**PV:** T14, T15, T18, T19, T27, T39, T40, T64, T65, T71, T81, T83, T84, T89,

T91, T111, T118, T127

**PS:** T35, T43, T61, T65, T73, T81, T89, T111, T118, T119, T127, T135

**TW:** T15, T19, T27, T35, T43, T61, T65, T73, T81, T89, T127, T135

**CE:** T15, T18, T19, T20, T24, T25, T26, T27, T29, T32, T34, T35, T39, T40, T43, T58

**MI:** T15, T19, T27, T35, T42, T61, T65, T73, T127, T131, T135

**CI:** T15, T19, T27, T35, T36, T43, T61, T65, T73, T81, T89, T107, T111, T119, T127, T131, T135

**Sing a Song, PV:** T14, T30, T34, T50, T76, T79, T110; **PS:** T34, T39, T46, T64, T76, T110, T142; **TW:** T18, T34, T39, T50, T64, T80, T96, T106, T110, T126, T142; **CE:** T18, T26, T28, T34, T47, T51, T64, T80, T85, T92, T95, T96, T106, T108, T110, T126; **MI:** T18, T26, T30, T34, T64, T76, T110, T126; **CI:** T18, T34, T38, T53, T84, T85, T93, T96, T99, T111, T122, T127, T128, T145

**Speak in Complete Sentences, PV:** T14, T15, T18, T20, T22, T34, T35, T37, T38, T39, T42, T43, T44, T47, T49, T51, T64, T66, T67, T68, T69, T70, T71, T75, T77, T81, T86, T88, T89, T92, T106, T107, T110, T111, T114, T118, T119, T126, T127, T134, T135; **PS:** T14, T15, T18, T19, T22, T23, T24, T26, T27, T30, T31, T34, T35, T42, T43, T46, T47, T60, T61, T64, T65, T68, T69, T72, T73, T74, T76, T77, T80, T81, T86, T88, T89, T92, T106, T107, T110, T111, T114, T118, T119, T126, T127, T134, T135; **TW:** T14, T15, T18, T19, T22, T23, T24, T26, T27, T30, T31, T34, T35, T42, T43, T46, T47, T60, T61, T64, T65, T68, T69, T72, T73, T74, T76, T77, T80, T81, T86, T88, T89, T92, T106, T107, T110, T111, T114, T118, T119, T126, T127, T134, T135; **CE:** T14, T15, T18, T19, T22, T23, T24, T26, T27, T30, T31, T34, T35, T42, T43, T46, T47, T60, T61, T64, T65, T68, T69, T72, T73, T74, T76, T77, T80, T81, T86, T88, T89, T92, T106, T107, T110, T111, T114, T118, T119, T126, T127, T134, T135; **MI:** T14, T15, T18, T19, T22, T23, T24, T26, T27, T30, T31, T34, T35, T42, T43, T46, T47, T60, T61, T64, T65, T68, T69, T72, T73, T74, T76, T77, T80, T81, T86, T88, T89, T92, T106, T107, T110, T111, T114, T118, T119, T126, T127, T134, T135; **CI:** T14, T15, T18, T19, T22, T23, T24, T26, T27, T30, T31, T34, T35, T42, T43, T46, T47, T60, T61, T64, T65, T68, T69, T72, T73, T74, T76, T77, T80, T81, T86, T88, T89, T92, T106, T107, T110, T111, T114, T118, T119, T126, T127, T134, T135

**Speak to Take a Telephone Message, PV:** T49

**Tell/Retell a Story, PV:** T28, T37, T67, T69, T82, T83, T85, T90, T97, T131; **PS:** T20, T51, T52, T62, T65, T74, T82, T99, T119, T120, T128; **TW:** T16, T28, T44, T82; **CE:** T28, T36, T39, T73, T74, T75, T81, T82, T89, T108, T120, T128; **MI:** T28, T36, T51, T120; **CI:** T28, T37, T44, T66, T97, T135

**Tell Jokes and Riddles, PS:** T18, T20, T36, T79; **TW:** T61; **MI:** T25, T67

## Understand Concepts of Print

**Directionality (see Track Print From Left to Right)**

**Identify Punctuation Marks (Period, Question Mark, Exclamation Mark), PV:** T61, T66, T74; **PS:** T20, T23, T69, T112, T123, T131; **TW:** T86, T122, T131; **CE:** T16, T28, T86, T120, T122, T132; **MI:** T66, T69, T86, T122, T132; **CI:** T16, T30, T31, T76, T86, T122, T131, T132, T144

**Recognize Letter, Word, Sentence Boundaries, PV:** T14, T23, T30, T40, T44, T46, T69, T76, T77, T92, T94, T111, T115, T124, T140; **PS:** T23, T69, T69, T76, T86, T92, T115, T132, T138; **TW:** T23, T30, T40, T46, T69, T76, T86, T92, T132, T138; **CE:** T23, T30, T40, T46, T69, T76, T122, T132, T138; **MI:** T20, T23, T30, T40, T46, T69, T76, T82, T92, T122, T132, T138; **CI:** T20, T23, T30, T40, T46, T69, T76, T82, T86, T92, T115, T122, T132, T138

# Index

Sentence Strips, **PV:** T38, T40, T69, T76, T86, T132; **PS:** T30, T40, T46, T76, T92, T110, T112, T122, T138; **TW:** T30, T40, T46, T76, T84, T92, T114, T122, T132, T138; **CE:** T30, T46, T76, T86, T92, T122, T138; **MI:** T40, T92, T115, T122, T132, T138; **CI:** T23, T30, T40, T46, T86, T132

## Viewing

**Demonstrate Active Viewing Skills/Visual Literacy,** **PV:** T39, T85, T131; **PS:** T39, T85, T131; **TW:** T39, T85, T131; **CE:** T39, T85, T131; **MI:** T39, T85, T131; **CI:** T39, T85, T131

## Writing

### Phonetic Development

**Associate Print With Spoken Language, PV:** T16, T20, T24, T28, T36, T39, T44, T62, T66, T70, T74, T82, T85, T90, T108, T112, T116, T120, T128, T131, T136; **PS:** T16, T20, T24, T28, T36, T39, T44, T62, T66, T70, T74, T82, T85, T90, T108, T112, T116, T120, T128, T131, T136; **TW:** T16, T20, T24, T28, T36, T39, T44, T62, T66, T70, T74, T82, T85, T90, T108, T112, T116, T120, T128, T131, T136; **CE:** T16, T20, T24, T28, T36, T39, T44, T62, T66, T70, T74, T82, T85, T90, T108, T112, T116, T120, T128, T131, T136; **MI:** T16, T20, T24, T28, T36, T39, T44, T62, T66, T70, T74, T82, T85, T90, T108, T112, T116, T120, T128, T131, T136; **CI:** T16, T20, T24, T28, T36, T39, T44, T62, T66, T70, T74, T82, T85, T90, T108, T112, T116, T120, T128, T131, T136

**Represent Sound/Symbol Relationship, PV:** T39, T44, T70, T85, T108, T120; **PS:** T16, T36, T39, T62, T74, T82, T85, T90; **TW:** T16, T22, T68, T74, T114, T120, T130; **CE:** T16, T22, T36, T39, T53, T66, T74, T82, T90, T114, T131; **MI:** T14, T15, T16, T17, T20, T31, T36, T38, T39, T44, T47, T77, T93, T123, T131, T136, T139; **CI:** T68

## Written Expression

### Pictures

**Draw Picture for a Response, PV:** T16, T17, T20, T25, T28, T29, T32, T36, T38, T39, T44, T47, T62, T66, T70, T74, T82, T85, T86, T93, T94, T108, T110, T115, T120, T125; **PS:** T15, T16, T18, T20, T25, T33, T37, T38, T41, T43, T48, T51, T62, T63, T65, T66, T71, T74, T81, T82, T86, T87, T90, T99, T112, T117, T119, T120, T131, T132, T137; **TW:** T17, T20, T25, T28, T37, T40, T44, T53, T66, T67, T69, T75, T81, T83, T86, T90, T94, T108, T113, T115, T117, T120, T128, T131, T132, T136, T137, T140; **CE:** T19, T28, T36, T37, T40, T41, T44, T67, T69, T74, T81, T82, T83, T85, T90, T91, T106, T108, T111, T112, T116, T120, T121, T124, T127, T128, T132, T133, T136; **MI:** T17, T19, T20, T23, T25, T28, T29, T31, T37, T40, T44, T53, T62, T66, T73, T74, T78, T80, T82, T83, T86, T87, T90, T91, T94, T99, T108, T111, T112, T120, T121, T122, T128, T129, T132, T133; **CI:** T15, T20, T21, T25, T28, T29, T39, T40, T41, T45, T52, T53, T63, T66, T67, T68, T70, T71, T74, T78, T82, T83, T86, T87, T90, T91, T108, T112, T115, T116, T117, T120, T133, T136

**Draw Picture to Tell a Story, PV:** T20, T29, T41, T83, T115, T129, T136; **PS:** T48, T74, T82, T83, T87, T90, T99, T128, T133, T143; **TW:** T28, T36, T44, T82, T115, T117, T132, T136, T137; **CE:** T19, T28, T36, T44, T74, T82, T91, T112, T120, T124, T136; **MI:** T37, T40; **CI:** T37, T48, T68, T70, T82, T87, T90, T91, T120, T121, T136

## Writing Forms and Genres

**ABC Book, PS:** T30, T47, T60, T61, T77, T93, T106, T107, T123, T139; **TW:** T14, T15, T31, T47, T60, T61, T62, T77, T93, T108, T123, T128, T136; **CE:** T14, T15, T31, T47, T82, T93, T123, T139; **MI:** T14, T15, T16, T17, T31, T38, T47, T77, T93, T123, I139; **CI:** T31, T47

**Autobiography, PV:** T20, T116, T145

**Cards/Letters, PV:** T74, T131; **TW:** T99; **CI:** T74

**Charts, PV:** T83, T97, T119; **PS:** T16, T37, T65, T80, T81, T86, T91, T97, T106, T111, T131, T143; **TW:** T16, T39, T51, T53, T97; **CE:** T14, T143; **MI:** T21, T50, T51, T71, T90; **CI:** T15, T39, T51, T81

**Poetry/Song, PV:** T62; **TW:** T90, T133; **CE:** T36, T85

**Recipe, PS:** T90; **TW:** T36, T85, T99

**Sign-In, PV:** T20, T99

**Signs, PS:** T44, T136; **CI:** T62

1. **Independent Writing, PV:** T16, T20, T23, T28, T32, T36, T40, T44, T48, T62, T66, T69, T74, T78, T86, T90, T94, T108, T112, T115, T120, T124, T128, T132, T136, T140; **PS:** T16, T20, T23, T28, T32, T36, T40, T44, T48, T62, T66, T69, T74, T78, T86, T90, T94, T108, T112, T116, T120, T124, T132, T136, T140; **TW:** T16, T20, T23, T28, T32, T36, T40, T44, T48, T62, T66, T69, T74, T78, T86, T90, T94, T108, T112, T115, T120, T124, T128, T132, T136, T140; **CE:** T16, T20, T23, T28, T32, T36, T40, T44, T48, T62, T66, T69, T74, T78, T82, T86, T90, T94, T108, T112, T116, T120, T124, T128, T132, T136, T140; **MI:** T16, T20, T23, T28, T32, T36, T40, T44, T48, T62, T66, T69, T74, T78, T82, T86, T90, T94, T108, T112, T115, T120, T124, T128, T132, T136, T140; **CI:** T16, T20, T23, T28, T32, T40, T44, T48, T62, T66, T69, T74, T78, T86, T90, T94, T108, T112, T115, T120, T124, T128, T136, T140

2. **Personal Journal Writing, PV:** T16, T20, T23, T28, T32, T36, T40, T44, T48, T62, T66, T69, T74, T78, T86, T90, T94, T108, T112, T115, T120, T124, T128, T132, T136, T140; **PS:** T16, T20, T23, T28, T32, T36, T40, T44, T48, T62, T66, T69, T74, T78, T86, T90, T94, T108, T112, T116, T120, T124, T132, T136, T140; **TW:** T16, T20, T23, T28, T32, T36, T40, T44, T48, T62, T66, T69, T74, T78, T86, T90, T94, T108, T112, T115, T120, T124, T128, T132, T136, T140; **CE:** T16, T20, T23, T28, T32, T36, T40, T44, T48, T62, T66, T69, T74, T78, T82, T86, T90, T94, T108, T112, T116, T120, T124, T128, T132, T136, T140; **MI:** T16, T20, T23, T28, T32, T36, T40, T44, T48, T62, T66, T69, T74, T78, T82, T86, T90, T94, T108, T112, T115, T120, T124, T128, T132, T136, T140; **CI:** T16, T20, T23, T28, T32, T40, T44, T48, T62, T66, T69, T74, T78, T82, T86, T90, T94, T108, T112, T115, T120, T124, T128, T132, T136, T140

3. **Shared Writing: Writing Dictated Stories, Class Books, Group Charts, Labeling, PV:** T16, T20, T24, T28, T36, T39, T44, T62, T66, T70, T74, T82, T85, T90, T108, T112, T116, T120, T128, T131, T136; **PS:** T16, T20, T24, T28, T36, T39, T44, T62, T66, T70, T74, T82, T85, T90, T108, T112, T116, T120, T128, T131, T136; **TW:** T16, T20, T24, T28, T36, T39, T44, T62, T66, T70, T74, T82, T85, T90, T108, T112, T116, T120, T128, T131, T136; **CE:** T16, T20, T24, T28, T36, T39, T44, T62, T66, T70, T74, T82, T85, T90, T108, T112, T116, T120, T128,

T131, T136; **MI:** T16, T20, T24, T28, T36, T39, T44, T62, T66, T70, T74, T82, T85, T90, T108, T112, T116, T120, T128, T131, T136; **CI:** T16, T20, T24, T28, T36, T39, T44, T62, T66, T70, T74, T82, T85, T90, T108, T112, T116, T120, T128, T131, T136

**Write a Story Innovation,** PV: T82, T121; **PS:** T70, T82, T116; **TW:** T28, T70, T74; **CE:** T20, T24, T82, T108, T112, T120, T131; **MI:** T82, T128; **CI:** T16, T66, T128

**Write About Information Books,** **TW:** T62; **MI:** T16, T20, T24, T36, T37, T39, T44, T51, T66, T70, T85, T90, T108, T112, T116, T120, T128; **CI:** T20, T24, T39, T82, T90, T108, T116, T131, T136

**Write Compound Words,** **TW:** T66

**Write Descriptive Words,** PV: T20, T39, T90; **PS:** T28, T29, T39, T42, T74, T80, T123; **TW:** T36, T106; **CI:** T44

**Write Name,** PV: T41, T49, T61, T77, T79, T91, T95, T117

**Write Rhyming Sentences/Phrases,** PV: T36, T62, T109; **TW:** T90, T133; **CI:** T120

**Write Sentences,** PV: T120; **PS:** T24, T36, T62, T83, T90, T93; T16, T20, T24, T28, T36, T39, T44, T62, T66, T70, T74, T82, T85, T90, T108, T112, T116, T120, T128, T131, T136; **TW:** T24, T70, T108, T112, T116, T120, T131; **CE:** T16, T24, T74, T90, T116, T136; **MI:** T28, T79, T131, T136; **CI:** T24, T27, T68, T70, T84, T108, T112, T114, T116, T130, T131

**Write Verses to a Familiar Song,** PV: T36; **CE:** T85; **CI:** T85

# Integrated Curriculum Activities

## Center Workshops

**Alphabet,** PV: T17, T33, T63, T79, T95; **PS:** T17, T33, T45, T49, T63, T95, T109, T125, T141; **TW:** T33, T49, T79, T91; **CE:** T63, T79, T125; **MI:** T49, T79, T125; **CI:** T33

**Art,** PV: T33, T41, T67, T75, T83, T87, T91, T109, T117, T121, T125; **PS:** T17, T21, T25, T29, T37, T41, T49, T63, T67, T71, T75, T83, T87, T109, T113, T117, T121, T129, T141; **TW:** T17, T29, T41, T63, T71, T83, T91, T109, T113, T121, T125, T129, T141; **CE:** T17, T21, T33, T37, T45, T60, T75, T83, T91, T117, T121, T129, T133, T137; **MI:** T17, T21, T29, T37, T41, T63, T67, T83, T91, T113, T117, T129, T133, T141; **CI:** T21, T29, T45, T63, T71, T75, T91, T109, T113, T121

**Blocks,** PV: T141; **PS:** T41; **TW:** T75; **CI:** T17, T41, T83, T133

**Cooking,** PV: T109, T121, T137; **PS:** T79; **TW:** T37, T45, T63, T71, T87, T113, T117, T121, T125; **CE:** T45, T95; **MI:** T137

**Dramatic Play,** PV: T21, T41, T49, T71, T87, T113, T137, T141; **PS:** T75, T79, T125, T129; **TW:** T37, T79, T133; **CE:** T17, T29, T41, T137; **MI:** T67, T91; **CI:** T17, T71, T75, T109, T117, T137

**Games,** PV: T25, T29, T45, T63, T91, T125; **PS:** T33, T71, T103, T113, T137; **TW:** T45, T95; **CE:** T41, T75, T109, T121, T133; **MI:** T41, T95; **CI:** T49, T79, T95

**Health & Fitness,** PV: T37; **TW:** T33, T49; **CE:** T125; **MI:** T109; **CI:** T113

**Listening,** PV: T25, T67, T79, T133; **PS:** T25; **CE:** T33, T113; **MI:** T79; **CI:** T79

**Math,** PV: T17, T71, T75, T83, T95, T113; **PS:** T21, T29, T87, T121, T137; **TW:** T17, T21, T25, T83, T95, T109, T129, T141; **CE:** T49, T67, T83, T117, T141; **MI:** T45, T75, T87, T125; **CI:** T29, T67, T95, T117, T121

**Music & Movement.** **PS:** T95; **TW:** T67, T75; **CE:** T25, T29, T79, T87, T95; **MI:** T33, T63, T71, T129; **CI:** T129

**Ongoing Project,** **CI:** T17, T21

**Science,** PV: T37, T129; **PS:** T37, T45, T67, T91, T117, T133; **TW:** T29, T137; **CE:** T21, T25, T37, T49, T67, T71, T91, T113, T141; **MI:** T21, T25, T29, T33, T45, T83, T113, T117, T121, T133, T137, T141; **CI:** T21, T25, T45, T67, T87, T129

**Social Studies,** PV: T21, T129; **TW:** T25, T41, T67, T87; **CE:** T87; **MI:** T71; **CI:** T63, T83, T91, T133, T137

**Writing,** PV: T29, T45, T49, T117, T121, T133; **PS:** T83, T133; **TW:** T41, T117, T133; **CE:** T109; **MI:** T25, T49, T87, T95, T109; **CI:** T25, T33, T41, T49, T87, T125, T141

## Connections

**Science,** PV: T82
**Social Studies,** **CI:** T62

# Everyday Literacies

## Research and Study Skills

**Follow Directions (see Follow Directions under Demonstrate Active Listening Skills)**

**Graphs,** PV: T75, T95, T113; **TW:** T21, T25, T95; **CE:** T66; **CI:** T29

**Maps,** **PS:** T71, T85, T87, T134; **MI:** T17; **CI:** T85, T131

**Use Parts of a Book,** PV: T16, T23, T62, T78, T79, T115, T125; **CI:** T69

**Use Reference Sources,** PV: T29, T45, T71, T85, T107, T133; **PS:** T14, T33, T37, T45, T63, T99; **TW:** T18, T87, T109; **CI:** T21, T29, T63, T71, T87, T88, T109, T118

## Kindergarten Concepts (ALSO SEE Acquiring World Knowledge)

**Colors,** **PS:** T23, T25, T32, T39, T41, T49, T66, T86, T94, T121, T124, T131, T133, T137; **TW:** T14, T17, T32, T48, T61, T64, T78, T81, T94, T109, T116, T132, T140, T141; **CE:** T47; **MI:** T67; **CI:** T118

**Days, Months, Year on Calendar,** PV: T72, T73, T75; **TW:** T18–T20; **CI:** T29, T89

**Numbers,** **PS:** T120, T132; **TW:** T129, T132; **CE:** T49; **MI:** T73, T74, T75

**Opposites,** PV: T43, T45, T65; **PS:** T26, T28, T43; **TW:** T36; **CI:** T64

**Positional Relationships,** PV: T16, T22, T34, T38, T60, T65, T92; **PS:** T115; **TW:** T35; **CE:** T79; **CI:** T43

**Shapes,** **PS:** T18, T21, T23, T137; **TW:** T17, T45, T71, T75, T81, T109, T141; **CE:** T15, T33, T45, T47, T106; **MI:** T21, T26, T29, T65, T67, T75, T141; **CI:** T75

**Transportation,** PV: T69, T71; **PS:** T85; **CI:** T14, T15, T60, T63, T106, T132

# Index

## INSTRUCTIONAL ISSUES

# Index

## Journal Opportunities

**PV:** T16, T20, T23, T28, T32, T36, T40, T44, T48, T62, T66, T69, T74, T78, T86, T90, T94, T108, T112, T120, T124, T128, T132, T136, T140

**PS:** T16, T20, T23, T28, T32, T36, T40, T44, T48, T62, T66, T69, T74, T78, T82, T86, T90, T94, T108, T112, T116, T120, T124, T128, T132, T136, T140

**TW:** T16, T20, T23, T28, T32, T36, T40, T44, T48, T62, T66, T69, T74, T78, T86, T90, T94, T108, T115, T120, T124, T128, T132, T136, T140

**CE:** T16, T20, T23, T28, T32, T36, T40, T44, T48, T62, T66, T69, T74, T78, T82, T86, T90, T94, T108, T112, T115, T120, T124, T128, T132, T136, T140

**MI:** T16, T20, T23, T28, T32, T36, T40, T44, T48, T62, T66, T69, T74, T78, T86, T90, T94, T108, T112, T116, T120, T124, T128, T132, T136, T140

**CI:** T16, T20, T23, T28, T32, T36, T40, T44, T48, T62, T66, T69, T74, T78, T86, T90, T94, T108, T112, T116, T120, T124, T128, T132, T136, T140

## Mentors

Chapin, Tom, **CI:** T6, T11, T57, T103
Mora, Pat, **CE:** T6, T11, T57, T103
Powell, Steve, **MI:** T6, T11, T57, T103
Twumasi, Kwaku, **TW:** T6, T11, T57, T103
Wada, Honey, **PV:** T6, T11, T57, T103
Wible, Becky, **PS:** T6, T11, T57, T103

## Places

Gardening Center, **MI:** T99
Performance Stage, **CI:** T99
Restaurant, **TW:** T99
Storytelling Corner, **PV:** T99

## Projects

"All About You and Me in School," **PV:** T145
"Animals Say Hello" Big Book, **CE:** T43
Big Book of Family Members, **PV:** T99
Big Book of Menus, **TW:** T145
Big Book of Recipes, **TW:** T99

## Modify Instruction

### ESL/ELD

### Extra Help

### Gifted & Talented

## Cultural Perspectives

## Technology

### Listening Center Audiocassettes

### Other Technology

### Phonics Audiocassettes

### Scholastic Network

### WiggleWorks Plus

### Video

# Literature

## Genre

### ABC Books

*A Was Once an Apple Pie*, **PV:** T14–T16, T38–T40, T60–T62, T106–T108
*ABC Drive*, **CI:** T14–T16, T60–T62, T106–T108
*Alphabatics*, **CE:** T14–T16, T60–T62, T106–T108
*Amazon Alphabet*, **MI:** T14–T16, T60–T62, T106–T108
*Apples, Alligators and Also Alphabets*, **PS:** T14–T16, T60–T62, T106–T108
*Eating the Alphabet: Fruits and Vegetables from A to Z*, **TW:** T14–T16, T60–T62, T106–T108

### Concept Books

*100th Day of School, The*, **TW:** T18–T20, T22–T23
*City Sounds*, **CI:** T80–T82
*From Head to Toe*, **MI:** T64–T66, T68–T69
*I Like Me!*, **PV:** T118–T120
*I Went Walking*, **PS:** T64–T66, T68–T69
*Mice Squeak, We Speak*, **MI:** T26–T28
*Over on the Farm*, **MI:** T72–T74
*What Am I?*, **PS:** T18–T20, T22–T23

### Emergent Readers

#### My Books

*Animal Sounds*, **PV:** T140
*Banana Bread*, **MI:** T32
*Empty Box, An*, **TW:** T78
*Getting Ready*, **PS:** T78
*Hair*, **PS:** T48
*I Can Be*, **PV:** T32
*I Can Draw*, **CE:** T124
*I Can Too*, **PV:** T48
*I Read, You Read*, **TW:** T140
*I Run*, **CE:** T78
*I Spy!*, **MI:** T78
*In the Garden*, **CI:** T140
*In the Nest*, **CI:** T78
*In the Park*, **TW:** T32
*It's Playtime!*, **CE:** T48
*Let's Walk*, **MI:** T94
*Listen!*, **CI:** T48
*Little Plant*, **MI:** T124
*"Meow," Said the Kitten*, **CE:** T32
*My Family*, **PV:** T94
*My Name Is Sam*, **CE:** T94
*Our Snowman*, **TW:** T94
*Our Town*, **CI:** T124
*Time to Get Up!*, **PS:** T94
*Too Small*, **MI:** T140
*Under Your Feet*, **CI:** T94
*We Clean Up*, **TW:** T48
*We Dance*, **TW:** T124
*We Like Food!*, **PV:** T124

*We Like to Build*, **CE:** T140
*Where Did They Go?*, **PS:** T124
*Where Is My Cat?*, **PV:** T78
*Who Can Help?*, **PS:** T140
*Who Is Ben?*, **PS:** T32
*Who Needs a Tree?*, **CI:** T32
*Zoo Sense*, **MI:** T48

#### High-Frequency Reader

*Band, The*, **TW:** T70, T86
*Big*, **MI:** T116, T132
*Can You See It?*, **CE:** T70, T86
*Dogs*, **TW:** T24, T40
*I Am*, **PS:** T10, T40
*I Can See*, **PS:** T70, T86
*I Like*, **PV:** T116, T132
*In the Forest*, **CI:** T24, T40
*Kittens*, **PS:** T116, T132
*Look!*, **MI:** T70, T86
*Lunch*, **PV:** T70, T86
*My Cats*, **MI:** T24, T40
*School*, **PV:** T24, T40
*We Are Painting*, **TW:** T116, T132
*We Can Go!*, **CE:** T24, T40
*We Like Fruit*, **CE:** T116, T132
*We Like to Play!*, **CI:** T70, T86
*What Is It?*, **CI:** T116, T132

#### WiggleWorks Books

*Birds on Stage*, **PS:** T34–T36
*Boots*, **PS:** T80–T82
*Clifford, The Big Red Dog*, **CE:** T80–T82
*Let's Get the Rhythm*, **CE:** T34–T36
*Miss Mary Mack*, **PV:** T34–T36
*My Garden*, **MI:** T126–T127
*Pizza*, **TW:** T126–T128
*Tortillas*, **TW:** T34–T36
*Tree Can Be, A*, **MI:** T80–T82
*What Lila Loves*, **PV:** T126–T128

## Fantasy

*Carlos and the Squash Plant*, **PS:** T88–T90
*Chrysanthemum*, **PV:** T26–T28
*Clifford, The Big Red Dog*, **CE:** T80–T82
*Corduroy*, **PS:** T118–T120, T143–T144
*Cow That Went Oink, The*, **TW:** T42–T44
*Herman the Helper*, **TW:** T26–T28
*Minerva Louise at School*, **CE:** T118–T120
*Mouse Mess*, **CE:** T42–T44
*Tale of Peter Rabbit, The*, **MI:** T134–T136
*Where's My Teddy?*, **PS:** T42–T44

## Fiction

*Abuela*, **CI:** T72–T74
*Blueberries for Sal*, **TW:** T118–T120

# Index

# Credits and Acknowledgments

## TEACHER'S EDITION

### Acknowledgments

Grateful acknowledgment is made to the following sources for permission to reprint from previously published material. The publisher has made diligent efforts to trace the ownership of all copyrighted material in this volume and believes that all necessary permissions have been secured. If any errors or omissions have inadvertently been made, proper corrections will gladly be made in future editions.

**Cover:** Linda Helton for Scholastic Inc.

**Sentence Strips:** Text for sentence strips adapted from PIZZA PARTY by Grace Maccarone. Text copyright © 1994 by Grace Maccarone. Published by Scholastic Inc. All rights reserved.

**Source Cards:** Plan 3/Side 2: "Jamboree" from ONE AT A TIME by David McCord. Copyright © 1965, 1966 by David McCord. Reprinted by permission of Little, Brown and Company.

**Book Credits:** Cover and spot art from THE 100TH DAY OF SCHOOL by Angela Shelf Medearis, illustrations by Joan Holub. Illustrations copyright © 1996 by Joan Holub. Published by Scholastic Inc. Cover and spot art from BLUEBERRIES FOR SAL by Robert McCloskey. Illustrations copyright © 1948, renewed copyright © 1976 by Robert McCloskey. Published by Scholastic Inc., by arrangement with Penguin Putnam Inc. Cover and spot art from THE COW THAT WENT OINK by Bernard Most. Copyright © 1990 by Bernard Most. Published by Scholastic Inc., by arrangement with Harcourt Brace & Co. Cover from EATING THE ALPHABET by Lois Ehlert. Copyright © 1989 by Lois Ehlert. Published by Scholastic Inc., by arrangement with Harcourt Brace & Co. Cover and spot art from HERMAN THE HELPER by Robert Kraus, illustrations by Jose Aruego and Ariane Dewey. Illustrations copyright © 1974 by Jose Aruego and Ariane Dewey. Published by Scholastic Inc., by arrangement with Aladdin Paperbacks, an imprint of Simon & Schuster Children's Publishing Division. Cover and spot art from JAMAICA TAG-ALONG by Juanita Havill, illustrations by Anne Sibley O'Brien. Illustrations copyright © 1989 by Anne Sibley O'Brien. Published by Scholastic Inc., by arrangement with Houghton Mifflin Company. Cover and spot art from JAMBERRY by Bruce Degen. Illustrations copyright © 1983 by Bruce Degen. Published by Scholastic Inc., by arrangement with HarperCollins Publishers. Cover from PIZZA by Saturnino Romay, illustrated by Annie Mitra. Copyright © 1994 by Scholastic Inc. Published by Scholastic Inc. Cover and spot art from PIZZA PARTY by Grace Maccarone, illustrated by Emily Arnold McCully. Illustrations copyright © 1994 by Emily Arnold McCully. Published by Scholastic Inc. Cover from SIONE'S TALO by Lino Nelisi, illustrations by Elspeth Williamson. Illustrations copyright © 1992 by Elspeth Williamson. Published by Scholastic Inc., by arrangement with Ashton Scholastic Ltd. Cover and spot art from THE STORY OF CHICKEN LICKEN by Jan Ormerod. Copyright © 1985 by Jan Ormerod. Published by Scholastic Inc., by arrangement with Lothrop, Lee & Shepard Books, a division of William Morrow & Company, Inc. Cover and spot art from TORTILLAS by Margarita González-Jensen, illustrations by René King Moreno. Copyright © 1994 by Scholastic Inc. Published by Scholastic Inc.

## Photography and Illustration Credits

**Photos:** Photo Stylists: Gayna Hoffman, Shawna Johnston. p. T6: Kwaku Twumasi for Scholastic Inc. p. T15: David Mager for Scholastic Inc. p. T16: David Mager for Scholastic Inc. p. T17: David Mager for Scholastic Inc. p. T19: David Mager for Scholastic Inc. p. T21: David Mager for Scholastic Inc. Randy Rodriguez for Scholastic Inc. p. T25: Ana Esperanza Nance for Scholastic Inc. Bie Bostrom for Scholastic Inc. p. T27: David Mager for Scholastic Inc. p. T29: Bie Bostrom for Scholastic Inc. Ken O'Donoghue for Scholastic Inc. p. T32: David Mager for Scholastic Inc. p. T33: David Mager for Scholastic Inc. © Stouffer Enterprises/Animals, Animals. p. T35: Chris Trayer for Scholastic Inc. p. T37: David Mager for Scholastic Inc. p. T41: David Mager for Scholastic Inc. Ellis Herwig/Rhonda B. Lindle for Scholastic Inc. p. T44: Clara Von Aich for Scholastic Inc. p. T45: Clara Von Aich for Scholastic Inc. p. T48: David Mager for Scholastic Inc. p. T49: David Mager for Scholastic Inc. p. T50: Ana Esperanza Nance for Scholastic Inc. p. T52: David Mager for Scholastic Inc. p. T53: David Mager for Scholastic Inc. p. T82: David Mager for Scholastic Inc. p. T83: David Mager for Scholastic Inc. p. T87: David Mager for Scholastic Inc. p. T90: David Mager for Scholastic Inc. p. T91: David Mager for Scholastic Inc. p. T94: David Mager for Scholastic Inc. p. T95: David Mager for Scholastic Inc. p. T96: David Mager for Scholastic Inc. p. T98: Ana Esperanza Nance for Scholastic Inc. p. T99: Chris Trayer for Scholastic Inc. p. T106: Randy Rodriguez for Scholastic Inc. p. T107: David Mager for Scholastic Inc. p. T109: David Mager for Scholastic Inc. p. T112: David Mager for Scholastic Inc. p. T113: David Mager for Scholastic Inc. p. T116: Clara Von Aich for Scholastic Inc. p. T117: David Mager for Scholastic Inc. p. T118: © S. J. Krasemann/Peter Arnold. p. T119: Chris Trayer for Scholastic Inc. p. T121: David Mager for Scholastic Inc. p. T124: David Mager for Scholastic Inc. p. T125: David Mager for Scholastic Inc. p. T127: David Mager for Scholastic Inc. p. T128: David Mager for Scholastic Inc. p. T133: David Mager for Scholastic Inc. p. T134: David Lawrence for Scholastic Inc. p. T136: David Mager for Scholastic Inc. p. T140: Clara Von Aich for Scholastic Inc. p. T141: David Mager for Scholastic Inc. p. T142: David Mager for Scholastic Inc.

**Upfront pages:** All reduced facsimiles of Student Anthologies, Teacher's Editions, ancillary components, and interior pages are credited, if necessary, in their original publication format.

**Illustrations:** p. T39: Gayna Hoffman for Scholastic Inc. p. T52: Ava Deluca-Verley for Scholastic Inc. p. T137: Colin Williams for Scholastic Inc.

Name

a  b  c  d

e  f  g  h

i  j  k  l

m  n  o  p

q r s t

u v w x

y z a e

i o u

small
letters

Copyright © Scholastic Inc.

**Teacher Note:** The above picture cards are: bat, bee, bus, cat, coat, cup, dog, duck, fan, fish, fox, leaf, lip, log, man, moon.

**Teacher Note:** The above picture cards are: mop, nest, nose, nut, pan, pen, pig, ring, rock, run, six, sock, sun, ten, tie, top.